When Lightning Strikes Your Child

And how finding the magic in everyday life will get you through the storm

KELLY CANNON

You've got this!
Kelly xo

TSPA
THE SELF PUBLISHING AGENCY

Nick

Kelly Cannon
When Lightning Strikes Your Child:
And how finding the magic in everyday life will get you through the storm

Shorewood Press

Hardcover ISBN 978-1-7383196-1-9
Softcover ISBN 978-1-7383196-2-6
eBook (Kindle) ISBN 978-1-7383196-0-2
Audiobook ISBN 978-1-7383196-3-3

Book Design | Angela Campbell
Editor | Alison Whyte
Author Portrait Photography (back cover) | Laura Elizabeth Portrait
Publishing Support | TSPA The Self Publishing Agency, Inc.

Dedication

For the boys in my life—my husband, Darren; my sons, Clive and Nicky; and my brothers, Jason and Ryan—without whom I would not be who I am today.

A Love Letter

On the surface, everything appeared to be in good health – not just in my child, but in my marriage. That's how life often unfolds; not everything is as it first appears. But as I've discovered, when appearances deceive us, it opens the door to countless possibilities—the chance to view things from any perspective we choose, to write the story we want told.

It gives us the power to speak our truth.

When a crisis crashes into a family's world, it can send lightning bolts through our cores, causing cracks to expand in our foundation and fires that quickly burn down our facades. We often find ourselves speaking harsh words we never would have uttered before, making decisions that were once unthinkable, and witnessing behaviours in ourselves that would typically be out of character in everyday situations.

Stepping onto the BC Children's Hospital cancer ward for the first time was like stepping into the purest form of truth humanity can offer. I encountered families as they truly were, met people in their most vulnerable moments, and witnessed raw, genuine emotions that didn't ask to be hidden. This was no place for dishonesty. In that truth, I found a strength I had never imagined possible and came to understand that truth is our most precious possession. It's the truth of who we are and the arduous journey we've navigated that can inspire courage in others—the way it had inspired courage in me.

As I slowly began to draw back the curtains and allow others to glimpse the reality behind the veneer, I discovered a wellspring of courage within myself—a courage nurtured within the walls of the hospital, a courage I had seen and admired in all the mothers who came before me. As this book unfolds, I delve into some of the most challenging moments of our journey, including the painful trials within our relationship and sides of my husband and I that we are not proud of. I believe that it is only in revealing this truth, uncovering some of the raw realities of childhood cancer beyond the ward, that I may fulfill my aspiration to be a source of courage in a world often clouded by fear—a world that believes in covering up the most unvarnished forms of our humanity or turns its back on those who need our help the most.

So, this book is my love letter—to BC Children's Hospital and its staff, to our families, to our incredible community, and to all those who held us together when we were falling apart. I do my very best to name as many people as I can throughout this book—my thank you for being the courage and strength I needed on the days I struggled to find my own. We were shown the very best of humanity, and I'll never forget it or ever stop paying it forward. It is my wish that you, my dear reader, will feel a steadiness in my words, gaining a deeper understanding of the paradoxes in your own life's journey: how the greatest strikes of lightning, which bring us to our knees, can also be the catalysts for our personal growth, allowing us to bend down and hold others who have fallen on theirs when we've found our way back up.

I hope my story will show you how to make every moment count, help soften the hardness that is childhood cancer, and symbolize for you the profound choice we all face when life's walls close in around us: Do you accept those walls as forces intent on crushing you or as sturdy arms and hearts inviting you to lean on them until you discover the deep courage you've always had within? That is the question of this book, and my offering for a brighter future.

I love you.

Kelly Cannon

TABLE OF CONTENTS

PREFACE

What is *The Flash*? It's a TV show, beloved by my son and many people of all ages. As luck would have it, it was filmed in our city of Vancouver, BC. I'll give you the synopsis from Wikipedia for reference.

> Barry Allen is a forensic chemist with a reputation for being very slow, and frequently late, which frustrates his fiancée, Iris West. One night, as he is working late on a new case, a lightning bolt strikes and shatters a case full of unspecified chemicals, drenching Barry, and temporarily knocking him out. As a result, Allen later finds that he can run at superhuman speeds and possesses equally enhanced reflexes, senses, and healing. He later dons a red bodysuit, sporting a lightning bolt in the chest, dubs himself The Flash, and becomes Central City's resident costumed crime fighter and protector.[1]

1 "Flash (Barry Allen)," Wikimedia Foundation, last modified September 15, 2023, https://en.wikipedia.org/wiki/Flash_(Barry_Allen).

Why is this relevant? Because throughout our experience with childhood cancer, I have found signals—crazy obvious signs and connections—that we were not alone in our endeavour to save our son Nicky's life. The world is a crazy place, but the universe works just as hard as we do to take care of us in every detail and assure us that we can make it through. The Flash helped Nicky respond to the lightning strike in his own life. With this fictional character as a guide, my son was able to morph his fear into courage and to build his own identity as a hero—while learning to believe in the impossible.

CHAPTER 1: THE BEFORE

I knew something was up. As I walked the dog at our neighbourhood beach, trying to get our daily steps in, I realized I couldn't ignore it anymore. I'd been married for eleven years, but for the last six I hadn't felt happy, connected, or fulfilled. It was spring 2021, and the COVID-19 pandemic had taught me some important lessons. Namely, that you can only depend on yourself for the truth. These walks by myself had taken the place of my volunteering at BC Children's Hospital, BCCH; they were where I found myself and some sanity.

As I walked on the seawall, Vancouver's scenic oceanside walkway, I reflected on the time I had spent in therapy and the guidance I had received from friends and family. At the same time, I realized I had a newfound trust in my own intuition. I put one foot in front of the other and enjoyed the calm I had finally begun to feel. I had consulted lawyers about my marriage, and where many would feel fragile, delicate even, I felt empowered. I'd finally found my voice and within it I had found faith in myself—it was stabilizing and gave me the invisible strength of an oak tree. I took comfort in this knowledge that I could take on the world. In fact, I reveled in it. I could sit in uncertainty, and yet I was confidant I would figure out how to navigate it.

As the week continued, I walked the same route and counted my steps. Gradually, in addition to this sense of peace brought on by my newly discovered personal strength, I started to sense something else. I had a feeling that something was coming—that I needed to brace for the impact of a storm.

Despite the trouble in our marriage, my husband Darren and I decided to take our kids, twelve-year-old Nicky and eight-year-old Clive, up to Whistler Mountain for a few days. On the last day of school before Spring Break, we picked them up from school. They both came trotting towards the car dragging their backpacks behind them. Clive rounded the car quickly, but I noticed that Nicky was limping slightly. I got out of the car and collected his bag from him. I brushed his carefully coiffed hair off his forehead and asked if he was hurt. He brushed it off as a result of playground play and said that he was fine.

Red flag.

We started on our drive up to Whistler, but soon pulled over. We wanted to film our boys' reactions as we delivered their acceptance letters to the prep school they'd worked incredibly hard to get into. It was a joyful moment, and it set the tone for the drive. With everyone singing and laughing, we headed to our cabin. After we arrived, we ate a quick dinner—and then Nicky asked for a hot bath to help his back.

Red flag.

As I drew the bath for him, it occurred to me that over the last two weeks, Nicky's requests for a hot bath had become more frequent. I left him to the hot water in the privacy every twelve-year-old boy hitting puberty asks for. After, he asked for a pain reliever, explaining it was still for the playground injury, and went to bed.

Red flag.

Saturday morning arrived and the forecast could not have been better—it was going to be a perfect bluebird day. Excitedly, I woke the kids. Nicky asked if he could stay back as his back hurt too much. I knew that he and his skiing instructor had had a disagreement the week before, so I figured he was just trying to avoid seeing him. I asked if another pain reliever might get him through the day, and he said it would.

That morning was epic. Our cabin faces the mountains, and their white peaks stood out against the sky, which was lit a bright reddish pink as the sun rose. It would be a perfect ski day—a ten out of ten.

I have had several injuries to my neck over the years and hadn't skied in a year. But that morning, the mountain, the sky, the snow—they just would not take no for an answer. We dropped the kids at their respective lessons and then I looked at Darren and said, "I have to ski."

Darren's mouth dropped open in disbelief and he responded, "Yeah, well why wouldn't you?" We hurried home to gear up and get our passes organized and up we went.

The day was perfect; the lineups were not too bad, and the air felt so good against my skin. As I inhaled, each breath energized my body and filled me with joy. I felt truly present. I reveled in the ache of my muscles as the day moved from morning to afternoon. It seemed like it had been forever since I had enjoyed cutting edges and feeling the icy snow beneath my sliding feet. We skied a total of four hours together and didn't have a single argument. Enjoying each other's pensive—perhaps apprehensive—company, we played nicely together in the sandbox for the first time in a long time. For my part, I tried not to be a nag on the hill or take offense to his competitive nature; he tried to be kind, pointing out the icy spots and waiting at the bottom of the hill more patiently than he normally would.

At 2:00 pm, it was time to head over to pick up the kids. Darren wanted to ski down. With my injuries, I superstitiously never ski the last run. We agreed to meet at the bottom. He took off and I headed towards the download lineup. As I stood in solitude and took in the view, I took a few more deep breaths. I organized my thoughts and began to take my skies off. That's when I heard it.

"Mommy! You're skiing!" It sounded like an angel. I turned, and there he was, my Nicky. I will never forget his smile and his pure innocence in that moment. I will remember it with wonder and gratitude for as long as I live. We took a couple photos together, smiling and laughing, and then I said I'd see him down at the bottom. "Okay," he said. He looked perfect. So perfect.

We all found each other at the base, and then decided to get back on the hill for one more glorious run together. After that, we packed up and headed back to the cabin. Everyone was so happy. Everything seemed so perfect. Our dog Sparky, jumping up and down, greeted us when we arrived, and Darren took him outside to pee. Nicky snuck off upstairs and began to run a bath.

Red flag.

We had plans to meet some friends for dinner that night, but Nicky wanted to stay home. Darren and I began to argue about whether he should have to go or not. I offered to stay at home with him, but Darren said he wouldn't allow it. We arrived with multiple pain relievers, and our friends offered to give him back rubs, thinking it was just a pulled muscle. Nothing worked.

Darren finally conceded that something was up. We decided we would head down first thing in the morning and organize a doctor's appointment for him. Later, near midnight, I heard rustling from my little guy's room. I went to check on him and found him crying that his back hurt and he couldn't sleep. I realized that he'd been tired for the last couple weeks, but I had assumed it was just a mix of moodiness and hormones.

Red flag.

We arrived home on Sunday. Nicky was in a good mood and so was Clive. Darren and I asked them if we could leave them for an hour so we could go grab lunch by ourselves. They were relaxing and playing on their screens, so they didn't mind. We got in the car and went to Joe Fortes, a steak and seafood restaurant in Vancouver. I don't really remember anything too exceptional about that lunch except the carrot cake. *It* was the absolute best carrot cake I had ever tasted. The cream cheese icing, cinnamon, and nutmeg—I indulged and allowed my senses to savour every bite. Darren enjoyed the chocolate cake and his glass of wine. It was a good afternoon. We didn't argue or fight and the small talk was pleasant. It would be our last carefree meal for a long time.

CHAPTER 2: THE HIT

Monday, March 15, 2021

Morning arrived and I got the boys packed in the car. We all loped into the waiting area of our GP's office with masks over our faces and sanitizer on our hands. I was worried it might be a kidney infection. In fact, I was pretty sure that was what it was based on the pain he'd been describing, and although he had been acting a little bit odd, my worry wasn't crazy high. At that point, I was sure the doctors would figure it out.

We entered the room and Nicky hopped up on the table. He explained his symptoms to the doctor and showed the spot where it hurt. The doctor looked over his vitals and then warmed up his hands and placed them on Nick's abdomen. And then he paused. He took his time checking the area over and over and over. He paused again, smiled, and said he was just going to ask his associate to come take a look. The next doctor came into the room, and they conferred, muttering and murmuring to one another briefly. The first doctor nodded and said, "Okay, thanks." Then, he turned to me. "Okay Kelly, I'm going to send you guys for an ultrasound. I'm going to put on the requisition form that there's a mass in the tummy. I don't want you to worry too much as I'm putting it there to get you in fast. Okay?"

"Okay," I responded. My mind clung to a naive sense of safety. I simply trusted the doctor's words. I didn't worry. I drove both boys over to the ultrasound clinic east of our place. With all the COVID-19 systems in place, we had to wait outside, and we weren't exactly dressed warmly. I let them wait in the car where I could see them and waited the forty-five minutes alone outside until we were let in.

We entered, sat for another ten minutes, and then were ushered into the exam room. Once again, Nicky hopped up on the table. The technician smeared jelly onto his belly and moved across it with her instrument and then she typed—click, click, click on her keyboard. After about fifteen minutes, she told us to wait there and that she'd be back. When she returned, she asked me to go with her to speak to the radiologist. I followed her to where the radiologist sat. It was a hallway. The boys were just eight feet away, sitting and spinning in the office chairs that lined the walls.

"I want to show you this," the radiologist said, as she pointed to a section of the scan. "This is cancer. And this here? This is cancer." She pointed to a few spots on the scan looking at me to make sure I was registering the importance of what she was saying. "You need to go to the hospital right away. You need to take this seriously."

I held my hand up and firmly said, "Stop!" In what world does a radiologist discuss a diagnosis like this within hearing distance of the child?! "I'll take it from here," I told her. "Will you let my doctor know? I'll need to get in touch with him. I need to tell my husband," I said.

Looking back, I realize this woman's intention was to make sure I did not waste any time at all, but in the moment, I was stunned. I asked the technician to watch the boys for a second and pretended to go to the bathroom. My mind was racing a million miles a minute and yet it also felt like it was at a standstill. I remember thinking, "How am I supposed to react to this? Should my reaction be sobs? Cries? Should they be loud? Soft?" I wondered. "I don't know. It should be tears, right?" I was in shock. I stared at my reflection for a few minutes and then dialed my husband's number.

"Darren." My tone didn't allow for any hesitation or questions. "Darren, I need you to come home. They're saying it's cancer. You need to come home now. I need you." My voice was calm but littered with shock and I believe it was at an octave I don't usually hit.

As tears began to fill my eyes and heart, I choked them down. I looked at my reflection in the mirror and told myself to keep it together. In that moment, I knew it wouldn't matter if I cried or not. No sob was going to relieve the pain and panic I was feeling. I gathered my kids as calmly as I could, but they knew something was desperately wrong. We headed home. I didn't have the answers to any of their questions. All I could say was that I needed to chat with our GP before we planned our next move. But I knew that day, in that moment, nothing would ever be the same again.

As soon as we got home, I immediately called our GP, and he explained the plan of action. He told me to try to get some sleep and that he would have a team assembled at the hospital ready to hit the ground running the next day at 8:30 am. I started to pack: pillows, snacks, a phone charger, pjs, notepad, pen, and Rudolph—Nicky's stuffed reindeer. Nicky had stopped sleeping with Rudolph by his side at that point, but I knew it would be the one thing he would grab if he needed to feel reassured. As I rushed around organizing things, Darren watched me.

"You don't need to bring all that," he said. But I ignored him. I was following my instinct, my intuition. I had volunteered on *that* floor of the hospital for seven years. I had experience. I knew. And I knew he did not understand.

That night, I cradled my children in my bed. They cuddled together tenderly and ever so quietly fell asleep, snuggled in each other's arms. It was the most beautiful tapestry, our limbs all woven together, our breathing in sync. I trusted the voice deep inside of me that told me this would be the last of these sleeps with my children for a very long time. So, I took it all in. I breathed in the tops of their heads, and I ran my fingers through their hair. I touched their foreheads and cheeks with my lips. As they purred in their sleep, I untangled myself from their grips and headed over to their room where I found Darren lying in Clive's bed.

He was wide awake. With neither of us saying a word, we put our differences aside. I got in beside him, and like the children did with me in my bed, I hid from our world in his arms. Silence can be deafening. I knew he felt my hot tears on his torso. I could feel the fear steam off his body and condense on my own. There was nothing to be said that would make this okay. Nothing. After an hour of just being there, I realized where I needed to be. Darren would have to learn to get along on his own now. We were entering survival mode. I got up, and Darren let me. I hurried back to the kids and re-entered the jigsaw that is my favourite place to ponder life's mysteries—their arms. That night, my search for the meaning of life was profound and endless. So were my tears, my fears, and my love.

CHAPTER 3: THE BLUR

Tuesday, March 16, 2021

The next morning, I packed the car. I think the kids hugged each other, but honestly, I was so stressed I am not sure. I took Nicky to the emergency room at the hospital as I had been instructed to do. As our GP had promised, they were expecting us. We were ushered into our own space, and it began: vitals were taken, and questions were asked. My child responded with timid but honest answers, aware that his worst nightmare was about to unfold. Needles, surgeries—he hates anything that can poke.

I remember when he was five years old and we were at our pediatrician's office for a checkup. It was time for the kids' vaccinations, and I'll be damned if that kid didn't run out of the room, through the waiting room, and out the office door. He ran clear down the hallway to the elevators and began to bang on the button screaming, "They're trying to kill me!" All the while in his underwear. I had to fireman carry him over my shoulder past the other businesses in the building and back through the waiting room where the other tiny patients waiting to be seen sat wide-eyed in fear at what could possibly be happening in there. He got the poke and within seconds said, "Oh. That wasn't so bad."

First things first: Nicky needed an IV. He had had one at the beginning of the school year for a broken arm, and he did not like it. His anxiety began to rise. I could sense it in all the questions he started asking as they wasted no time setting up for scans and tests. The IV needed to happen. Magic cream, also known as Emla numbing cream, was applied, and Nicky got a heating pad for his arm. As we moved through all these actions, one steady energy was a nurse named Kyle. He wore a bandana as a headband and had a gentleness, a kindness, that Nicky gripped onto instantly. Nicky instructed everyone that only Kyle was allowed to put in his IV. They all tried to give as much control to Nicky as possible as he was tumbling down the rabbit hole of fear.

Kyle's first attempt was a failure. He couldn't find a vein. He stopped and told us to hold on before disappearing briefly. He reappeared with a woman that *only* does IVs. Nicky began to object but his new, trusted friend explained that he was not going to put him through anything that he could prevent. He explained to Nicky that this lady was so good, it would be over before he knew it. As she started to set up, Nicky's anxiety was rising and so were his attempts to stall the procedure. He clung to me in fear. She asked him to count to twenty. By the time he hit five, it was done. This woman was now a hero. A temporary relief set in, and it allowed us to catch our breath for a split second before we were whisked away for scans: an ultrasound, a CT, a nuclear scan (where they injected Nicky with radioactive dye to track the functioning of his kidneys), and an MRI. As we were leaving, Kyle came to my son's bedside, held his hand, and looked him in the eye. "You take care, little man, and good luck," he said. Then he turned to me. He knew. "I'm sorry you have to go through this," he said. He was calm and real. Where others tried to offer optimism or hope, Kyle provided steadiness. He was our anchor in the middle of a storm. It was exactly what I needed. It helped me keep my eyes focused on what was in front of me.

Kyle may not remember us, but every time we needed to visit the ER through this journey, my son asked for him. Kyle was in our life for a mere few hours, and yet the impact he left on us was profound and remained with us for the whole journey. Out of everyone we met on that first day, Kyle is the name that Nicky remembers. He was the centre of gravity we desperately needed when life attempted to hurl us into the stars and expected us to navigate our way to the moon. I will forever be grateful to Kyle, and Nicky will love him forever.

Hours passed and the day felt endless. It was as if we were in a holding cell awaiting our sentence. I think Darren brought us food. I think we spoke on the phone, and did we text? I honestly don't remember. I do know I was calm for Nicky, for Darren, and for Clive. Nicky kept looking at me for reassurance every few minutes, and the calm that I had felt for weeks was slowly oozing out of me. My adrenaline was racing in my body, but my spirit was still calm. It was as though there was a hand on my shoulder that whole long day. Finally, we were told that we were moving upstairs. I knew that this was coming. We were being admitted. That's why I packed our bag so carefully. It's why I was bracing for *that* button I knew I would recognize in the elevator—8. Up we went. *Ding!* Top floor.

The hallway I had not seen since the beginning of the pandemic encapsulated me. I walked through it in a trance. Familiar murals on the walls and faces I had so genuinely missed over the preceding months came into view. At first, they smiled at me excitedly as if to say, "Welcome back!" I watched as the realization of why I was there dawned on them, and their expressions changed to, "Wait, no!" The understanding that I was not there for my volunteer shift, that I was there as a mother, hit and we processed that information together in a split second of eye contact. The cheerful smiles flickered to looks of anguished understanding.

We rounded the corner, and I saw my friend standing at the entrance to a room. That's when I felt it all and I collapsed into a hug. I sensed my entire self break apart and finally feel safe. It was the sight of my friend that pulled the pieces of mè that had been holding steady to the edge, and I finally could feel the weight of the entire day. The threads that had held me together were stretched that bit thinner. I knew this doctor better than any other on the floor; I adored his wife and knew their family from Nicky and Clive's school. He was the one I respected with every cell in my body: Dr. Rod. The blur took over my mind as they set my Nicky up in the room. I lost what little reality I had been clinging to as I entered. I surrendered to it. I moved to the side and allowed Melanie, our nurse, and the assigned team take charge. I felt a presence within me, almost like a hand on my shoulder. It told me to have faith. Silently, I wiped the tears from my cheeks. At that moment, I knew there was nothing left for me to do but give in and trust.

I could not tell you what exactly happened after that moment. I know we had everyone on the team helping set up my child for success as scans were analyzed and IV tree poles were hooked up beside the bed. This team—they worked so hard and so gently to ensure Nicky was not in pain. We had kidney specialists, urologists, oncologists, and nurses. The nurses! They truly are the heartbeat of the hospital. But to try to remember precisely what occurred in those first few days is like trying to see a grey dog in the fog. I have to look at the photos I don't remember taking to dip my memory back in that pond. Nicky was still able to move around a bit the day after we were admitted, so we made sure to visit with Clive and Sparky outside. I'm so glad we did. That would be the last in-person visit Nicky would have with his sibling, pet dog, or outside life for seven weeks.

Nicky was on such high pain medication that he didn't look or act like himself. His lower limbs were swelling. He cried, hallucinated, and talked in his sleep. He'd yell things like "Clive, stop cheating!" or "Clive, come here!" while he slept. It was clear: he missed his best friend. Clive could not visit inside, so we would Facetime every day. But as the days progressed, Nicky would sleep more and sometimes miss his chance to talk with him. He missed all his friends. I'll never get over the heartache of that situation.

Dr. Butterworth installed a medcomp central line in Nicky's chest right above his heart. This device would allow the medical team to administer two IV treatments at the same time without having to repeatedly poke his sweet arms. I had to learn how to flush both lines, or lumens, and seal the system back up every night. I also had to learn how to change the dressing, which proved to be one of the most traumatic parts of this whole thing. The dressing for the medcomp line had to be changed every ten days, and every time, removing and cleaning the area involved ripping multiple layers of skin from Nicky's already fragile body and then dousing the area in alcohol to ensure it was cleansed properly. We would both brace ourselves for these days and wait until the absolute last possible minute to do it. Each time, I would let him help remove the bandage as he knew where it would hurt less and how fast to go. Imagine being entrusted to perform a procedure on yourself because it was so painful? Nicky became so tough and full of strength, far tougher than he should have been for a twelve-year-old. It wasn't fair.

Dr. Webber performed the biopsy on the tumour. Even though the incision was only three or four cm long, it proved to be a painful recovery. Nephrostomy bags were attached to both kidneys to allow his urine to drain directly out of his kidneys. This reduced the pressure and eased the swelling in his lower body, which was already under stress due to the tumour.

All the while, I struggled to explain to Nicky what was happening. But what could I say?

"A biopsy was taken of the lump inside your abdomen, Nicky. That means that the doctors took a little piece of the bump and are going to look at it under the microscope. From that little piece of the bump, they're going to be able to see what sort of medicine will fit with that puzzle piece. They'll be able to see the bad guy cells that are trying hard to take over and they'll know which soldier cells to send in. This helps everybody make a plan of attack on just those cells. Not you, just those cells. You have done nothing wrong."

As the bandages came off, scarring blisters were left where Nicky's beautiful, flawless olive skin had been. Slowly, the battle wounds began to accumulate. Slowly, the tan left from our Maui Christmas vacation was stripped away by all the adhesive on the bandages and dressings that were pressed on his perfect frame. Slowly, his skin was wrapped in the dull hue of illness. We waited for the specific diagnosis.

As the days progressed, I was made to witness the advancement of his symptoms. The swelling, the pain, it all hurt. We took an ambulance to have a PET scan at a nearby hospital and no matter how hard the paramedics and travel nurse tried to minimize them, the bumps and bangs from the stretcher as we drove on the uneven road caused tears to well up in his eyes and spill over. Any time he had to move from his bed, his body could not bend to his doctor's needs. Pain and anxiety and ache were always there, bubbling under the surface and heard in his cries. Always.

Right in the middle of this, they needed to remove Nicky's braces. I tried to arrange for his own orthodontist to do it, but I could not. The hospital dental department, in the basement of an older, connected building, was our only option. The swelling in Nicky's lower body had become so intense at this point that he could not use a regular wheelchair; he required a larger one. As we made our way down towards the dental department, I quickly learned that there are some incredible porters—people who move you from one department to the other either in a wheelchair or in a stretcher—and there are some people who do not belong near a hospital and I don't know how they were hired in the first place.

As we tried to get Nicky through a door but could not, the importance of advocating hit me. I had reached my limit and he had far passed his own. Here he was, already anxious about the braces coming off, and now a woman who could not differentiate between a child in a wheelchair and a bumper car madness ride was subjecting him to unnecessary pain. Then there was the impatient dental team not wanting to fall behind in their appointments. I noticed another mother and child in the room, but quickly moved to the task at hand. I took charge. I told the porter kindly but firmly that we would not need her services anymore and she was not to touch Nicky's chair again. I explained to the lady behind the desk that this wasn't an average boy: he was scared, nervous, in pain and above all, he was mine. I needed her help to get him into that dentist chair so that the dentist could do what he needed to do. I pleaded and begged. She looked at me, paused, and then she really saw me. I don't know how we did it. It was like a game of goddamned Tetris moving Nicky and the chair and then Nicky and then the chair. I held his hand and with the eye contact of a tiger I let him know he had nothing to fear. I would be his champion going forward. No one would go near his body again without my okay.

After much wincing and many tears, Nicky was in the chair, and the braces were off. Small win. As we finished up with my still very anxious, fear-filled child, I felt a tapping on my shoulder. I turned to see the lady from the desk.

"Would you like a cup of coffee?" she asked.

"What? No. Thank you, but no," I sputtered. I was so confused. After the intensity of this moment, coffee was not on my mind. It turned out that the offer actually came from the mother with the child in the waiting room. As we opened the door to the waiting room, I saw her familiar face. "How do I know you?" I wondered. I realized my eyes had spilled all the secrets that I had been trying to keep from Nicky, and she saw them. It was such an act of kindness—it took my whole heart and held it for a brief moment. Did she say she knew me? I can't remember, but the truth is her compassion grounded me. Silver linings and full circle moments would continue to appear between us, but this one is etched into my memory for all of time.

This woman, Lexi, noticed me. She saw me and acknowledged me when no one else did. She became a face I was grateful to see over the course of this road. We bonded over the chaos. She has remained a constant in my world— a friend and someone I am so proud to know.

CHAPTER 4: THE MEETING

As it turns out, I don't like meetings—especially the meetings we would have with Nicky's medical team. There was always way too much focus on the what ifs and the future. These meetings were meant to inform us and maybe even empower us, but personally, I felt that they took my eyes off the target and didn't allow me to stay in the present where I felt safe—safe with Nicky still beside me.

At this first meeting, I remember there were a lot of people in the room. We were all masked because of the COVID-19 pandemic, and I was finding my mask particularly suffocating that day. There was a lovely nurse, Maddie, who explained that she would be taking notes. I looked to Darren.

"I'll take notes too," he said.

"There will be a lot of information coming at you in this meeting," Maddie warned. "It's important that you focus on what the doctor is saying. I promise that I will take detailed, accurate notes for you."

I relented.

Dr. Rod began, "Okay, so we got the biopsy results back. It's called Desmoplastic small round cell tumour."

I've never heard of it. What's the name? I don't like it. Have I heard of it before? Déjà vu? No, I don't know this illness. Why does it sound so familiar? It's not. Desmoplastic small round cell tumour. Such a long name; it was like he was speaking a different language.

Dr. Rod continued. "The likelihood of being diagnosed with this specific tumour is 0.3 in 1 million. That means you are more likely to be struck by lightning three times than to be diagnosed with this specific sarcoma."

I remember thinking, "What are the chances that lightning chose to strike our family more than three times?"

Dr. Rod went on. "I'm not going to lie. Nicky is very very sick. If you had come in a few days later, we would *not* be having the same discussion." As it was, Nicky was nearly in organ failure. I think I asked what stage he was at. They explained it's different with kids. They don't focus on the stage, and we shouldn't either.

The meeting continued and Dr. Rod began to lay out the specifics. "Here is the treatment plan that we're beginning right away . . . Here are the good things we know . . . Here's what we don't like . . . Here's what we don't know . . ."

Darren remained laser focused on the team and what they were saying, but I don't remember a lot of this conversation. I do remember wondering if the walls were closing in on me, or if they were holding me up. "Why won't they just let me crumble? How are my legs still beneath me?" I wondered. I got up from the table, braced against the wall, slid down, and crumpled into a ball. "Damn these stupid COVID masks. They make it feel even more stifling," I thought to myself. I couldn't catch my breath. Would I ever catch my breath again? I thought I was going to be sick. My world was suddenly spiraling out of control. It was very loud in my ears even though I know the room was quite quiet. The room was spinning, but it wasn't spinning fast enough to knock me out entirely. I needed Darren to make it stop. I needed to go back in time. "Please," I begged silently. "Rewind this so we can fix it before we get to this spot. Someone, help!" There were a thousand voices screaming and shouting in my brain—different thoughts, opinions, emotions, but all with the same end goal: **Fix this. Make it stop.**

Slowly, I began to refocus on what was being said. I heard Dr. Rod say, "We're here to help. We're going to do everything we can to help Nicky. I'm your doctor, and I've seen this rare bump before. We followed this same protocol, and the boy is doing really well."

These words should have helped, and they did. But the comfort was so small compared to the agony we felt as we were thrown into this new world. I couldn't feel it; I couldn't absorb it. But I knew that Dr. Rod was going to captain our spaceship through this chaotic alternate universe. He was our pilot, and I knew I had to trust him implicitly, maybe even blindly. It was as though we had been faced with a field littered with land mines, and this team was tasked with getting us through it. I knew the team had the training and the skills to give us our best shot at survival. In that moment, I gave Dr. Rod the wheel.

"We're going for cure, and I don't say that if we can't try," he said.

Let's get to it.

CHAPTER 5: THE TRUTH

When this all began, my own Mama Bear instincts were to protect my child's body and spirit at all costs. As we learned the lingo of our diagnosis and what the treatment would entail, I recognized quickly that the vocabulary used around Nicky would have to be amended until he could handle it. And honestly, maybe around all of us until *we all* could handle it. The breakdown of his body was proving too much for his mind. I needed to simplify it all for him: he was sick; there was a bump in his abdomen that was making him feel bad. It was leaning on and blocking other things in his body, and it wasn't allowing them to work correctly and that's why things were hurting and swelling. We were going to use medicines to make him feel better. He was very sick, and therefore we would need to use really big and strong medicines, and yes sometimes they would have to be given to him through needles, but he could have a say as to when they went in, and we would use the "magic cream" (Emla numbing cream) to help it not hurt quite so badly.

There was one time when the doctors pulled me out of Nicky's room to discuss another addition to his treatment. I had posted a note on the door asking the medical team not to discuss anything in front of him. I wanted them to talk to me first. This way, I could censor the information and condense it down into something he could handle. After I returned to the room, Nicky asked me what they had discussed with me outside. I responded, rather sheepishly, with something noncommittal in an attempt to lessen his interest in the conversation. But when the nurses entered and needed to give him another needle, he lost it on me and called me a liar. The look that he gave me was filled with such deep pain. I had betrayed him, and a line had been crossed.

I begged for his forgiveness, and I vowed to him that I would never hide what would happen to him again. In my mind, I promised the vocabulary would still go through me, but I would make sure he knew what procedures were coming up. He had a right to know what we knew. His maturity was growing at a rapid pace, and he deserved to be a part of the conversations.

Since that time, Nicky has accused me of lying twice more, but I never have since. I can swear on my life that I have stayed true to my vow to him since that moment. I know that when he has broken down and yelled or picked a fight with me it has been because he was feeling vulnerable and sensitive, and I was the safe spot to lash out at. I am his safe spot, his blanket, his umbrella. I shield him from the storm, and it is my duty and privilege to do this for him.

For their part, the medical team agreed to use our special vocabulary. We used the word "bump" not "tumour" as it sounded less intrusive and more beatable. Darren and I made the decision not to reveal the actual name of the diagnosis—the type of cancer—to anyone. We decided to be vague so that no one could offer advice or look up potential treatments on the internet for us. I had seen how my own family reacted when older relatives experienced disease. With the best of intentions and out of a desire to help, the suggestions were often random.

"Did you try this algae?"

"I have heard aloe vera juice is wonderfully helpful to the gut."

"How about apple cider vinegar?"

I nipped that in the bud before it happened. I never even looked to Google for answers. Not once. I never tried to research statistics or random cures or even just common questions for people with cancer. As far as my search engine knew, we were cancer free.

We already knew the negative statistics any well-meaning family would find if they searched the internet for information about Nicky's cancer. I didn't need any non-experts chiming in about the odds of success for a treatment plan that I had entrusted to a world-class medical team. I wanted our team of specialists to lead the way. I had discovered that the statistics were meant only to guide medical professionals and their decisions about treatment. In the end, patients are not statistics; they and their bodies are unique and will react differently each time. Patients are not meant to involve themselves in the statistics; it's a language for the professionals to speak to each other. I had seen enough split in opinion in 2020 about the pros and cons of the new COVID vaccines. Through all that, people had no problem voicing their opinions using statistics without understanding them. That had no place in our journey.

We sent out the following blanket email explaining that Nicky was sick and what was happening for us at the time.

Hi everyone,

So, I thought I'd reach out at this point as word is getting around (mostly because Nicky now has his own phone), and I realize that we're in the most supportive cohort of all time.

We entered BCCH in a hurry on Tuesday and after CT scans, MRIs, blood work, and three procedures, we're embarking on a journey.

I'm gonna set it straight and let you, the parents of Nicky's closest friends, know what's up. We will fill the class in as time goes on (and yes, the school knows).

Our boy has been diagnosed with a rare form of cancer. We've got quite a battle ahead of us. He has a mass in his tummy and we're gonna need treatments beginning this week for it. We're surrounded by incredible doctors and staff. It happens that we're now staying on the ward where I have volunteered for the last seven years, so although we have no visitors thanks to COVID, I know so many people up here that we see familiar, kind faces, and there are people I can confide in and Nicky can trust.

What we would appreciate from the kids is humble, positive, honesty and compassion. We'd so appreciate it if everyone could avoid using the "C word." That said, if Nicky brings it up, then acknowledge it. We're not hiding from it and yes, he knows what he has. We are just trying to keep him in a healthy frame of mind. I have used the following wording to explain the situation to our youngest: "We have a bump in his tummy and we're gonna use all sorts of science and medicine to get rid of it."

Nicky is on quite a bit of pain meds right now. It's only been a short period of time, but he has been poked and prodded more than anyone I've ever seen up here. He's been incredibly brave and patient. Please, no scary talk or advice from Google searches on this one.

We love you guys, and I thank you ahead of time for your kind words and support. I am on autopilot now. I'm on a mission to be by his side and get him well. Darren is also on a mission; he's home with Clive and trying to keep his life on track. We trade off if we can for about an hour, but I'm here at the hospital 99% of the time.

We love you, and I appreciate your discretion. I will be in touch as to how the boys can support their friend. Or if you have great ideas, we'd love to create some cheer so feel free to organize some positivity. We know this is Nicky's and our battle, but I also know we've got an army behind us and a village full of love and friendship.

Thank you again, and lots of love. If I don't respond immediately, please don't take it personally. We will hopefully be sending updates. XO.

CHAPTER 6: WHY ME?

When we first entered the hospital, I couldn't eat. I had no appetite. My stomach would ache, and I'd get sick whenever I tried to eat something. I just couldn't stomach that my child was so ill. I couldn't accept my new viewpoint in this familiar place. I was no longer seeing the patient from the side where the volunteers enter and stand. I was now watching my son from the other side of the bed, where the parents sit.

"Why me?" Nicky would ask me in the darkest hours. I had no answers. How could life be so unkind, so cruel, that it would put him through his worst of fears and nightmares: needle pokes and surgeries? How could it take him away from his dreams and goals—the things that he had studied so hard for on his own initiative? How could it take him away from his friends and stunt his social growth just as he was entering the last year of elementary school? Why him, indeed.

I understood every emotion he was feeling. I was just as confused and outraged, and I think he understood that I couldn't explain it. When he asked me this question, I wondered what he needed from me in that moment. Love? He knew he had that. Trust? I knew he trusted that I was with him every step of the way. Then what?

I looked at my sweet child. His eyes have always been the most incredible, multi-coloured, mesmerizing place. I can always lose myself in them. They change with his mood and the colour of the sky: green-blue with yellow centres, lined with the darkest and thickest of lashes, which he clearly got from his Uncle Ryan. As I gazed at him, I realized he needed to feel heard. He needed to feel seen, to feel validated. He needed to know that everything he was feeling, whether it was a big or small feeling, was valid and real. He needed to feel like himself and to know he mattered.

So, when he asked me, "Why me?" I got as close to him as possible, cradling his fragile and slender yet swollen frame, and I said very simply, "I don't know. I don't have the answers. It's not fair. There is nothing about this that is right. You do not deserve any of this, and if I could make it better, I would in a second. What I do know is you are in the right place. I have been involved with this floor for over twenty years and working on it for seven, and I can tell you magic happens here, and I will help you see that every day. We'll have little miracles, little wins, every day as we edge you closer to your day of victory. I love you and no matter what you endure through this, I will always be by your side. You won't have to question this. I am here for you and with you."

I knew that, with this declaration, Clive, my then eight-year-old, had just become another victim of this cruel disease. I could have chosen to trade off with Darren, but I also knew that I alone could get Nicky through this. Seeing the good and finding the hope in dark places—this was my area of strength. This was my expertise. It was Darren's area of weakness. He was better suited to the task of staying steady as Clive's rock. I knew Darren would excel at cultivating a routine for Clive.

As the reality set in, I could feel years of resentment build up in my fists as the wave of unfairness hit my own heart. Darren is a good man. He's a great man, in fact. I wouldn't have married him or had children with him if I didn't see the potential in him and appreciate his attributes as a kind person. But like everyone out there, including myself, his faults began to show through in the hardest of times, as I'm sure mine did to him as well. It's not his fault. Like a tattoo etched onto your subconscious, your upbringing—the way you were raised—forms the blueprint for how you will treat others as an adult. When my husband was a child, he was taught not to discuss his feelings and never to appear vulnerable. He learned that if someone were to ever expose their vulnerability, he could one day use that against them as their weak link. To him, illness is embarrassing, inconvenient, and a sign of weakness. As his partner, I learned that if I were to come down with anything, I would be expected to get through it on my own—with as much dignity as I could muster.

When I suffered a serious neck injury, I had to drive myself to the emergency room, twice. I was told to stay essentially immobile for eight to twelve weeks, barely moving anything. I was prescribed serious pain medications and anti-inflammatories. I was delirious, but Darren showed little to no empathy. I didn't feel like I could ask him to drive me to my appointments, so I had to rely on girlfriends and doctor friends. A week after my diagnosis, he took the kids and went on our family trip to Maui, leaving me home alone. He promptly hired himself a nanny and had a lovely time. Years later, my neck is still the weakest part of my body.

More recently, an autoimmune attack of brachial neuritis hit me and paralyzed my right arm. I couldn't use it at all. My husband again left me to fend for myself. It was a lonely and steep recovery, but I got through it with the help of my friends. I think Darren knew I was at my breaking point because he finally managed to find the right words. But I was still waiting for the actions to back up the idea that I was important. Thankfully after many acupuncture appointments suggested by a dear friend, my arm healed with one month to spare before Nicky was diagnosed.

The emotional damage of these experiences imprinted on my brain, and I was on the brink of separating from my husband when this new trauma of cancer hit us. How could I leave Nicky with this example of care? I am sure Darren would have tried to step up in ways he had not before, but to all of us the choice was clear. I had to be Nicky's main caregiver to make sure he lived. And to do that I had to leave Clive with Darren. I had made it my mission to honour both of our kids' feelings in life and to provide them with a safe space to share their vulnerabilities. I wanted my boys to accept their feelings, not be ashamed of them, to feel free to express them and to grow up to be caring, empathetic men. I worried how Clive, at such a young and impressionable age, would fare without his mom.

Holy fuck, the mom guilt I felt! This, on top of Nicky's serious illness, my failing marriage, and the loneliness and isolation of the COVID-19 pandemic—it was all too much.

So, selfishly, I too asked, "Why me?" I had been doing the work. I had stayed true to my kids and had become strong in my sense of self. I was unhappy in my marriage, but I had sought therapy to discuss my faults and vulnerabilities. I had made an effort to try to address the problems, but sadly I was alone in that effort. I had finally made the move to empower myself; I met with lawyers and financial experts to educate myself. I learned that I didn't have to stay in this situation where I wasn't happy and didn't feel appreciated. I couldn't connect the dots. Why me? I certainly could not connect them to explain why this was happening to Nicky.

So then let's rephrase it.

Why not me?

We are not unique or special, no matter how our lifestyle or social status would have the world or our own egos believe. Nobody is. We have genetic, physical, mental, and spiritual flaws as much as anyone else in the world. But here's where I found my legs—not just to walk through this fire, but to run through it. I realized I had personally been training for this experience—this triathlon of childhood cancer—without ever knowing I was doing so, pretty much for all my life.

CHAPTER 7: HOW DID I GET HERE?

My greatest joy, my passion in life, has always been children, and I have naturally gravitated towards roles that involve them. Over many years, I held multiple positions at the North Vancouver Outdoor School. It remains my favourite workplace ever—my forever happy place. Every school term, hundreds of elementary children take a bus up to Paradise Valley Campus to immerse themselves in nature and learn about the great outdoors and the environment. Depending on their age, they stay in cabins with their classmates for two or four nights.

These cabins are led by volunteer camp counsellors who are high school students; the counsellors go through an incredible leadership program and develop skills and self-esteem they would never gain any other way. Many of these counsellors come to the camp weighed down by the pressures of high school where they may have been dealing with any number of issues. Some are labelled "nerds" or "not cool." Others are "too cool." The playing field is leveled as they are measured through the eyes of younger children instead of their peers. The counsellors pick out cool nicknames for themselves and suddenly "Mr. Not Cool" has a new alias he can go by for an entire week and feel the power of it. Everyone is a superhero! The excitement leads to mentorship and bonding that last forever.

Over the course of the week, the counsellors and their charges go on field studies to learn about the forest and the industry that affects it; or they focus on salmon studies, farm studies, or even the weather. They learn about all these topics, and at the same time they can twirl in the presence of old growth cedars and feel the splash of an old salmon trying to race up the stream to spawn; they can experience the excitement of releasing the fry into the streams in hopes they make it to the ocean.

This campus is situated in an area that has one of the largest concentrations of bald eagles in Canada. Through the fall and winter, you can look up and always count three to four eagles hovering around, looking to eat a spawning salmon. Or, you might find a stinky salmon on the forest floor, left by a predator to decompose—a great opportunity to show the kids how even that is a good thing since the nutrients from the dead salmon's body will be absorbed by the forest. Similarly, the trees that have fallen are still useful. As "nurse logs," they provide shade and vital nutrients to seedlings, thereby ensuring the continued health of the forest.

I'm sure it's obvious I'm still very passionate about this program. I experienced it first as a student, then as a counsellor, and finally as an intern working with the staff. It was there that I first worked with kids with special needs and challenges—some physical and some less physical. I watched in wonder as children diagnosed with ADHD, who had a hard time sitting in a normal classroom setting, excelled in classes where they were allowed to explore their thoughts. It was inspiring.

At one point, I was invited to train to be a team member for a boy on the autism spectrum. I excitedly accepted and eventually transitioned out of the outdoor school setting and began working as an Applied Behavioral Analysis (ABA) therapist. I fell in love with my kids. This was all in my early twenties. From there, I was offered a position as a youth care worker for children in foster care and felt an overwhelming need and calling. My last assignment weighed heaviest on my heart as I worked night shifts with kids in group homes. I was there to make sure they wouldn't hurt themselves. Suicide watch.

With every child I worked with, I felt growth, excitement, and peace within myself. I felt love for each of them. Helping them was my passion. Was it easy? I've had more demanding jobs at times. Was I good at it? I like to think I was.

Another serendipitous moment—a lightning strike of my own—came in 2000 when a high school boyfriend of mine landed a part on an MTV mocumentary TV series about boy bands called *2gether*. What was special about this was that Michael Cuccione, who also landed a part on the show playing a character named Q.T., had already battled Hodgkin's lymphoma twice and survived by the time that he joined the cast. Sadly, his respiratory system and lungs were never the same after all the treatments, and he lost his life to pneumonia at the age of sixteen in 2001. I had had the privilege of meeting Michael through my then boyfriend and enjoyed his sweet self and funny sense of humour. I attended his funeral and the annual galas that his family organized to raise money for childhood cancer research.

When I would walk into the clinic side of the ward at BCCH, I would see Michael's face as a giant picture of him hangs next to the playroom and there is a plaque highlighting his foundation for childhood cancer research. I have to admit, I was grateful to see a familiar face through it all, even though it was in the form of a picture hanging on the wall. I had been proud to say I knew him when I was a volunteer. I was even more proud when I would later introduce myself to his mother and father at a fundraiser and tell her our story. The hug and cry we shared meant a lot to all of us.

My involvement with BCCH began during my time with the outdoor school program. During the Christmas break, I would go with my fellow counsellors to decorate Ward 3B—oncology—in honour of my friend's beloved sister, Melinda Hathaway, who remained in the hearts of all the nurses long after her death. This became a happy tradition for over ten years for us as it naturally brought a group of friends together every year to remember the good times and continue a legacy for a family we all cared about. I thank this family every day for including me in their lives as it has helped me more than they may ever know. It was their love that introduced me to pediatric oncology. It was their grace that placed me on the floor amongst these child superheroes, and their kindness that inspired me to always be connected to this hospital through oncology.

We decorated the ward for the last time in 2008. I was very pregnant with Nicky and looked like Santa myself at that point. The hospital had announced a change in protocol for the ward, and so we knew this would be our last time. I savoured every moment. As I approached motherhood, I tucked away a seedling wish—to always be bonded to this floor and to help in any way I could.

In September 2015, two and a half years after our second child Clive was born, a two-year-old boy named Alan Kurdi was found washed ashore near the Turkish city of Bodrum. The image of this boy, who was the same age as Clive and resembled both my children, gave me a pain in my chest I could not equate to anything. Even the clothes on his lifeless body looked identical to the outfits I clothed my kids in. I felt the family's loss as my own. For weeks, I could not sleep and continuously cried openly about it, but the ache in my heart would not ease. At one point, I considered starting a fundraiser in this boy's name, but a voice inside me said this was not the way.

I decided to look a little closer to home for opportunities to help. I wanted to get my hands wet and dirty locally, so I got up the courage to apply as a volunteer to BCCH. I'd heard it might be a long wait, and I figured I'd need something to do in a year or so when Clive entered preschool. Whoops! They called me two weeks later for an interview. I was nervous as I'd been out of the workforce for a long time, but after chatting with Dana, the coordinator, I was confident she'd find me a great place within the hospital. She offered me a volunteer position as a family support worker. My job would be to look after the parents who couldn't leave their child's bedside: get them a cup of coffee, a blanket, a meal, toiletries, or even clothes if they had come in suddenly. Family support workers are there to listen and hold space for these parents as they process what transpires during the long nights and endless days. They are the wall the exhausted can rest upon—a guardian or keeper of sorts. Then, magically, I was given my floor to keep: oncology.

I loved my role on this floor. I believe I became my best self in this role. I made it mine. I wore a nametag that read "Ms. Thursday" (my shift was on Thursdays). I would wear funny headbands or hats to let the kids know that although I was a grownup, I was not a doctor or nurse, and I was not there to poke them with needles. I was there to check on their mommy or daddy. Could Mom and Dad use some help or support? Did they need anything at all? Did they just want to talk it out in a safe, nonjudgmental space? This is where I thrived!

I loved speaking with the kids, too. Teens were my favourite, particularly teenage boys. They reminded me of my own brothers, so I'd talk with them about "guy stuff": cars, trucks, sports teams—anything that might fall within the spectrum of male interests. But there was one teen who was different. He had the corner suite, and we would talk about Broadway shows. I loved chatting with him and his beautiful mother. New York was the goal for this one. His dream still matters to me, even today, and I hope and pray that it's been realized and achieved.

What I noticed right away was the children, perhaps up to the age of nine, endured with resilience. It was built into them. They knew they didn't feel well, and that's what their day would entail. But the older kids, especially the teens, they knew what they were missing out on. They'd had goals and dreams that had to be sidelined: sports teams, school trips, dating, learning to drive. These were social experiences that would pass, and they could not get them back. These were the kids I tried to connect with most as I believed those sad thoughts, lost dreams if you will, needed to be heard and validated. This was all before the COVID-19 pandemic when the experience of missing out became commonplace to all kids and teens during that time. Before then, it wasn't so recognized, and I wanted to help these kids know that their goals and dreams still mattered, and that they should hold onto them. Just because an expectation is not met, it does not make it go away, and it needs to be honoured.

One Thursday, I saw a familiar name in our notes for the day. I didn't connect the dots right away, but then I recognized her. It was my roommate from when I was in my early twenties—a sweet, lovely survivor of childhood cancer herself. She had beaten it in her early teens and battled wicked side effects from the treatment ever since. As time moved on, so did we, keeping tabs on each other with friendly hellos on Facebook. And then lightning struck, and she was back on the floor, this time with her own child. Her story is hers to tell, but here is the relevance to mine: I am so grateful I knew her before so that I could be there for her as she navigated and advocated for her child in the hospital. Fast forward another ten years and the roles reversed. She was instrumental in helping me grieve and one of the only people who truly understood my feelings without my needing to articulate them. She's the wisest and most informed lady for someone so young, and I am grateful that she was willing to be a part of my story and allowed me to be a part of hers.

It was serendipity. Lightning had struck on purpose for me to have walked this path for so long, and for all the right reasons. It was because of everything I learned working and serving as a volunteer with these kids and their families in oncology that I knew to lean into Nicky's child-like innocence. He followed my lead and I think it helped. He didn't feel the pressure to keep up socially with his peers or explore more mature thoughts and instead allowed himself to process through play. It was a big win thanks to what I had learned as a volunteer at BCCH.

My other volunteer space in the hospital was the Families in Recovery (FIR) Program—a special ward dedicated to helping new mothers who struggle with substance abuse issues. Here, in this private space, moms and babies can work through withdrawal together and hopefully figure out a path that keeps them together. It was here that I learned that judgement is a reflection of the person passing it, not the person it is directed at. I watched countless mothers who had endured trauma after trauma, who were simply dealt a bad hand in life, form a bond with their babies—the first true love they've probably ever known. I'd see the hope in their eyes that they could do this. They were realizing they were becoming more than they had ever been allowed to be. I watched the moms kiss their babies' foreheads, count their toes, and tickle their feet. They'd coo and smile and sing lullabies to their sweet ones just as I would to my own children. If you want to see real, true love, go watch these mothers. They are angels. More often than not, I'd see the heartache as these mothers would choose the strongest gesture of love. Because of the uncertainty of their own recovery, they'd decide to give up custody of their baby and have to watch it be placed in the care of a family member or foster parent. I can still feel their pain and their hope of one day reuniting with their children. It's sacred.

Canuck Place Children's Hospice in Vancouver was another program I was privileged to volunteer for. I worked in the kitchen during lunchtime once a week for a little over a year and would help prepare food for the chefs and assist with clean up afterwards. Interacting with the families at this position brought so much joy and light to my life. Even if they were there under the hardest of circumstances, there was a lightness, a respect, a calm acceptance of this beautiful thing called life. Again, I would leave with a perspective of blessings and realism of what this life is all about. I am so grateful for this experience.

I could go on and on about all the organizations I volunteered with as the list is extensive and there are many more not included here. I am proud of each and every one, but the point is to give insight into my heart and to explain the direction I was always heading and never knew. I am not special, and I am no more worthy of good luck than the next person. Life is practice and I had been practicing for what this ward holds, not fearing it. At that point in my life, after all I had seen as a volunteer, I was qualified, skilled, and experienced in what happens in pediatric oncology. I had seen the magic that the doctors and nurses make happen for the little people that need them. I had seen countless numbers of parents dig deeper than I thought possible to find the strength to continue on a road they had not mapped out for themselves. And somehow, I had always been riding alongside on that journey.

If Nicky had to be sick, then I was so glad he had me. I felt blessed to be his mother because I was not afraid of those hospital walls the way others might have been. I was confident in the medicine and science that occurs there. Plus, I believed I was destined to help children, including my own, to know deep down inside that they matter and that they have more strength, courage, resilience, and magic than they realize.

Let the lightning strike. Life has been paving a way through it for us all this time.

CHAPTER 8: THE VILLAGE

When I was a boy and I would see scary things in the news, my mother would say to me, "Look for the helpers. You will always find people who are helping."
— Mr. Rogers

It takes more than the parents to raise a child. It takes a village. That's the line everyone knows and finally believes once they have children of their own. After the diagnosis, rumors flew, but for the most part, people had the best intentions. The best in everyone came out, as they put their most positive foot forward to help us accept the hand we'd been dealt. The news spread like wildfire and so we had to either accept the heat, extinguish it, or comprehend how fire lives in all of us. We received calls, emails, and text messages from people I didn't even know. Old friends came out of the woodwork to let their voices be heard. I like to believe in the good in people. Here is what I have found. Bad news triggers something in all of us. It can spark fear, gratitude, and sometimes, even relief—the "I am so glad it's not me" reaction. It can even result in indifference, resignation, or a resurfacing of personal trauma. It's the car accident you can't take your eyes off of. As you drive by, you hold your breath, take it in, and mutter something. We got served all the mutterings. One could go on the offensive for these chatters, but the truth is, it's a solid prayer for oneself. Whatever emotion it ignites in your body, you breathe out in shock. We witnessed lots of different takes on the situation, whether we wanted to or not. People's intentions are usually good, but it's the impact that matters long term.

I really appreciate the optimistic people, the ones for whom the glass is always half full. These are the people with the hearts of gold that feel our pain and empathize with it and give us some space to hold it. These people send you all their good energy, their prayers, and their intentions. And truly, these things help. I felt them to my core.

In contrast, there are the glass half empty types, the pessimists, the ones that are unable to control the tears in their eyes.

"Oh my god I can't imagine what you're feeling, what you're going through."

"I don't know what to say. I'm so so sorry."

I know they meant well, but the more I heard these lines, the more they began to trigger me, and my interpretation of them changed in my mind. "What are you sorry for?" I'd think angrily. "Why are you pretending that you are unscathed by this flame inside our world right now? You are not. You can feel the heat. I know you can. You can see the damage it is leaving in its wake. You've been burned too. I can see it," I would think bitterly.

And then there are the people who are jealous of your glass entirely—the people who want the same attention you are receiving because of the ordeal you're enduring. It's gross. They pretend they are the answer to changing your glass. These people attach to your family, link their identity to yours, all in a bid to get some of the spotlight; this is the ugly side of things.

I know our family situation brings all the fear bubbling up to the surface for every family, even the self-serving, insecure ones. But we—Nicky, Clive, Darren, and I—had to deal with that fear and move past it every moment of every single day. The heat from this wreck was the momentum pushing us forward. In the end, we were simply grateful to have the glass—any glass at all.

I want to make special mention of the women who helped, the women who are like sisters. This fabric, this tapestry, somehow emerged and I didn't even realize how strongly it had been woven. Mothers. Mighty Mothers: moms of Nicky's friends; moms of Clive's friends; my own mom friends. They emerged and they rallied. They took the fear and moved past it with me and like a wave they came from behind and propelled us forward. They blanketed us in this cloth, knit together with every emotion, every hug, and every shared tear. It was fucking beautiful. It held me together when I was cold and coming undone at the seams.

Sometimes the waves were gentle. At other times, they were powerful riptides or even tidal waves. No matter the size, every single act of kindness was felt in our body of water and incredibly impactful on our world. Kindnesses appeared in so many different forms: meals, care kits, pajamas, flowers, pillowcases, token inspirational gifts, consistent messages and check ins (no reply expected), car rides, and play dates for Clive. Nicky's classmates carefully curated packages that would arrive every day he was in hospital. They were filled with letters, cards, games, books, comics, jokes, and inside information from one kid to another about what the scoop was on the playground. These packages were incredibly motivating and kept Nicky connected when he so easily could have lost contact with his fellow classmates. They got more and more elaborate as Nicky's treatment progressed. When he was receiving stem cell treatment, they included decorations for the room: signs, posters, and pictures exemplifying the comradery between Nicky and his friends. They even arrived for Clive. Every kid needs this.

One of my favourite people at BCCH is the head nurse in the ER, Marliss. She is also a mom, and her children attend the same school as Nicky and Clive. Over the years, I've gotten to know her and consider her a friend. Before the chaos of 2020, we would often grab coffee when on shift together and compare parenting notes. After Nicky was admitted, she brought me a keyboard to play in the room so that I could process everything that was happening in the only language I am truly proficient in: music. It moved me over the hurdles and helped me get to where I needed to be. She just intuitively knew that this would help me, and I'll always love her for it.

I was given another gift of things that, if I'm honest, frightened me. It was a giant gift bag of medical supplies. My friend Karen had been down the road of childhood cancer with her boy Hawken just before Nicky was diagnosed, and she knew exactly what I would need. I tucked it away, knowing I would use it and focused on her child's success as the goal. Hawken was healthy and had recovered in all ways. He came out swinging, surrounded by his classmates and loved and protected by my youngest, Clive, when they were in grade one together. Karen is easily one of the most kind and generous ladies I've had the privilege to have as a friend in my life and on this journey. There isn't a feeling that she hasn't experienced, that she doesn't recognize in me, and so to have her on my team meant everything to me, and it also had an important impact on Clive. Because Hawken beat it, cancer never scared Clive. Clive understood what illness looked like because he'd already witnessed it in his own best friend. He knew it would be a battle, but it was a battle that Hawken won so it never occurred to Clive that Nicky could have any other outcome. I will be eternally grateful to Karen and Hawken and their friendship and guidance throughout it all. They were the stars that gave us hope.

Another incredible gesture was made by my dear friend Ali, who organized a team of people to run in Nicky's honour in the RBC Race for the Kids, a family charity run sponsored by the Royal Bank of Canada that benefits BCCH. It's special as it has different lengths—2km and 5km—so it allows the whole family to participate. The goal for Team Nicky was originally $4000, but once our school heard about it and joined in, alongside our friends, family, and the community, it blew past that goal quickly. We raised a whopping $150,000! This was all because a neighbourhood came together for Nicky. Corrine, Jen, and Sara (moms of Nicky's friends) made signs to encourage the runners and made sure that everyone was dressed in the team colours: red and yellow of course, like The Flash! All his classmates were there, cheering one another on and propelling each other to the next marker. Clive ran for his brother alongside his own friends and in turn saw support for himself—our very own hero to follow.

Nicky was undergoing one of his earlier chemotherapy treatments during the run, and so he and I experienced it from his hospital bed. We sat there in our Team Nicky t-shirts that my father had made, glued to the internet and watching all the posts come in. Nicky saw how much people cared about him. There were wild pictures of screaming twelve-year-old girls and boys while signs with Nicky's name and "You've got this!" were hoisted into the air. Darren was there too, dashing from crew to crew and sporting a spandex costume of The Flash—albeit probably one size too small. Nevertheless, it was incredible to see Darren open up, take it in, and become the superhero Nicky believed in. It was special for me to witness Darren make that effort, too. It was pure magic and hope, all around.

Darren's friends helped us too. His colleague Dan Jordan and beautiful wife Jill championed a small fundraiser called Work Out to Conquer Cancer, a month-long fitness challenge to benefit BCCH. It began as a general email that circulated around the office with no personal details attached. But then one colleague dedicated a large amount in honour of Nicky and our family, and suddenly it took off. We marveled as it went over and above the goals again reaching $150,000. Nicky was even allowed to be a part of choosing where the funds were allocated in the hospital. A significant amount went to support the research being carried out by our own incredible oncologist; some went to social work to help as many children as we could, and the remainder was allocated to support mental health initiatives for children.

I've left the most special gesture for last. Five of Nicky's buddies took it upon themselves to surprise him during one of his many rounds of chemotherapy. They Facetimed us from a barber shop. They wanted him to know that they were giving him all their own strength and courage and standing with him through this journey. Each of them took their turn in the barber's chair and buzzed their hair dos away. He was so touched and moved by the act of solidarity. It was a big day in a lot of ways. Nicky had had to start isolating himself from his friends as a health precaution, but these kids and their families found a way around it.

As they hung up, they all promised, "See you later!" Nicky looked at me and explained that he had told them not to do it. But I could see, the nurses could see, we all could see what this had shown Nicky: that he wasn't alone in his fight. This selfless act assured him he would not be left behind, that they would always be friends, and that they were along for the ride. Nicky tried to hide the smile, but we all saw it curve on his sweet lips. He realized how much he mattered. It was a profound moment.

Ryan, Matthew, Imran, Laughlin, and Austin, my greatest wish is that you forever see the value of friendship and understand how an act of kindness can save a person's life. You did just that. You saved Nicky's spirit. Truly.

CHAPTER 9: THE TOOLBOX

Dig deep

It's primal. That's how I'd answer people when they asked how I was able to do it. It's the space you go to when you're in your worst nightmare and can't wake up from it. You have to face the monsters with whatever tools and skills you have, and they may or may not be enough. I've said this before, but I really do believe I had been training for my role in this journey—that of pediatric oncology caregiver—my whole life. I learned one of my most valuable lessons as a volunteer when I worked with a particular mother, Sammy, and her boy Samuel. They were residents on the oncology ward for nearly an entire year. He was just a baby when he arrived on the ward, and I was sure she was the same age as me. She always radiated love and peace. The room was never charged with chaotic or sad energy. Every day, I watched her in wonder as she fed her child homemade meals, hugging and cuddling him into giggles or sleep as he lay on her chest. She *never* left his side.

She became one of my favourites, and I loved to help her. I would do anything I could as I knew I was witnessing a special kind of strength in her. I remember arriving at her door one day and it was busy inside. I'd brought her regular order: a large hot chocolate with whipped cream and a muffin. I sensed it might not be a good day and my usual need to connect took a backseat. I realized in that moment that support does not always need to be seen to be known or felt. I quietly left her drink where she would find it and left without a sound. I pray she knows how much I loved her and her son from afar and continue to keep them in my thoughts and prayers. Sammy and her son are my heroes. I will forever be grateful to have witnessed their journey as it guided me through the troubled waters of my own.

These are some other tools that I discovered along the way.

Humour

When I was a volunteer at BCCH, I made friends with a beautiful woman named Meenakshi, and her feisty, smiley kid, Jihaan. When I was in the hospital with Nicky, a friend of ours brought a delivery of cookies to share with the ward. They were decorated with beautiful messages: "You've got this!" "Yes you can!" And, of course, lightning bolts. We had finished handing them out to everyone and were going to take a spin in the elevator. As we approached it, there was the beautiful mother and her smiley son. I grinned and introduced the boys to each other. Jihaan had no hair at the time.

"Hey, I like your hair do," said Nicky, with a grin. Jihaan paused and glanced uneasily at Nicky. Nicky took this moment to pull off his tuque, saying spiritedly, "I have the same one!" Both boys let out howls of laughter and from then on became allies in strength and understanding for each other. They continued a friendship shared in a dark humour from a wisdom known too soon.

Gratitude

I need to be grateful every day for every moment I get to spend with those that I love. As the incomparable Michael J. Fox once said, "With gratitude, optimism is sustainable."[2] When you wake up every day to a hellish situation with gratitude, you can lean into the fact that you're still fighting. With gratitude you realize that you have the opportunity to fight at all, and that after the fight, the bridge of love is stronger between you and your heaven because of the fight. I realized it's not my job to save him through this, it's my job to love him throughout it all. I was grateful for that opportunity every day then, and I will be every day after. I'm so grateful he's my child.

Compartmentalization

I always thought this was a male trait, but I needed to learn this one quickly. You can be given good or bad news, and you'll need to walk back in the room to be with your child or people and not share what's on your mind. I'd give myself five to ten minutes of privacy a day in the bathroom where I would allow myself to feel sorry for myself and experience all of my feelings. At the end of those minutes, I'd look myself in the mirror and say, "That's all the time for that. Don't waste any more time in here. Go out and make it count." I'd say bury it, but really, it's learning to put a pin in it and come back to it when you're able to process it. It's not an easy task, especially for parents or other caregivers. To be honest, there are still topics that I have yet to take the pin out of.

---

2 Michael J. Fox, interviewed by Jane Pauley, *CBS Sunday Morning*, April 30, 2023.

Processing

Everyone does this differently. The point is to sit with your feelings to allow them to move through you so you can acknowledge them but not hold onto them. Playing the piano or walking the beach in front of our cabin helped me process things. So did holding my children close, watching a movie with them, tickling them to hear their laughter, or watching them sleep. I quit drinking alcohol immediately as I knew I needed to be absolutely sober and present every second for Nicky and Clive, but my husband needed it to take the edge off of life. He needed to work out in the gym more, but I needed to become more still. Everyone is different. You'll figure out what takes your edge off. I appreciated having more of an edge as, strangely, it allowed me to feel more relaxed. I felt that if my edges were sharp, I wouldn't miss anything for Nicky and therefore it took the fear out of the moment, or at the very least dialed it back. I needed to feel connected to myself in every moment, and therefore I became very good at recognizing where I will find that vibration and where I will not, especially in my own body or in a room.

Unapologetic distraction

In the quiet times I had to myself, I no longer worried about appearing lazy or looking tired. If I needed to numb out on social media or listen to a podcast in my car, I'd take that opportunity with open arms when it presented itself to me. I knew I was not lazy; I was exhausted, and I would do whatever it took to recharge my batteries. It was necessary, and it was what I needed to survive.

Screams and songs

In the rare moments I could make it out of the hospital and down to my little car, I'd aimlessly drive down a street that was unfamiliar to me, put on the saddest song—one that would allow me to feel all of my emotions from the playlist I'd made just for these moments titled "All the Feels"—and finally scream. I would scream at the injustice and unfairness of it all. I'd allow for the lyrics to guide my emotions through the moments I needed to process. I'd allow the fear to fall down my cheeks or feel the hope swell in my spirit and help me to keep going.

Heart-shaped sunglasses

I bought myself a pair of chic, fancy sunglasses that were heart-shaped, not because they were fashion forward, not because they looked great on me or were in the least bit flattering, but because every time I put them on my face, I felt silly and light. It reminded me to laugh and giggle at myself. I would wear these and laugh over and over at myself and enjoy it. I advise anyone going through something like this to wear a silly hat or funny socks or something to remind you that a lightness does exist in your world, even if you need to create it for yourself.

Adrenaline on no sleep

People have often asked me what it felt like, and the closest thing I can compare it to is having a newborn. When a baby is born, you wake up in the middle of the night and muddle through responding to its cries: feeding, diapering, burping, cuddling to sleep. No matter how tired you are, you get it done, checking every few minutes to ensure the baby is still breathing in its basinet. After the first few weeks, you realize that you can do most of it on half a brain. When Nicky was sick and cried out for me, I'd wake up and go from zero to a hundred in a second. My brain needed to be completely on to handle whatever he needed for pain, sickness, bodily functions, or his mind. I never really slept. I could hear his breathing in my sleep and in the eleven months we were in and out of the hospital, I never dreamt. I never had one dream or nightmare. I can only assume that I never reached REM sleep. Friends gave me supplements to help with restless nights and although I'd try them, nothing would allow me to sleep for more than two hours in a row. I always woke up to make sure he was okay or to remind the nurses to be quiet when they moved through our room in the wee hours of the morning. I kept hoping for that feeling that all new mothers get, of knowing that they could do it with half a brain, but it didn't come. It never did. Instead, I learned a new skill: surviving through it on barely any sleep at all and always one hundred percent on when I woke up. There was no other option. It's simply survival mode—running on fumes and doing the best you can. My adrenals were shot. I compromised the health of my own body not by choice, but by necessity. My nutrition suffered as I ate whatever I wanted or whatever was available. Even now, I'm feeling the repercussions of those unconscious choices I made. However, I made a deal with the universe that it could do whatever it wanted with me if it would let my son have his health and live. I'd do it all over again.

Nicky became habituated to wake every four hours during the night when the nurses interrupted his sleep to check his vitals or, during the day, when the custodial staff would unintentionally bang into things as they mopped the floor or changed the garbage and laundry bag. He was on so many crazy medications that he would often hallucinate in his sleep. The IV machine would beep, signaling the need for the nurse; it would read "AIR IN LINE" and make this consistent beeping sound. Nicky, in his delirious state and assuming it was his alarm for school, would turn over and mumble, "Alexa off!" Often, he would sit up and talk to Clive. He'd be in an argument with him about some game. "Don't cheat, Clive. Stop cheating!" Sometimes, his arms would reach out into the air, and I'd hear him giggle and laugh, as if he was playing a game. "Clive! Ha ha ha!" and it would trickle off. It was always with Clive, and it broke my heart into a thousand pieces each and every time.

We were both severely deprived of sleep and although the people keeping us awake were medical professionals who were trying their hardest to help us, I couldn't help but realize that sleep deprivation was often used in other situations as a torture tactic. Although certainly not the intention of the people that tirelessly work those hallways, it was an unfortunate consequence of the actions needed to keep my child alive and lessen his pain. I'd give up sleeping for the rest of my days on earth if it meant that Nicky could sleep peacefully in a healthy body until he is a wrinkled old man. And while he was undergoing treatment, that's just what I did.

People would say to me, "I don't know how you are doing it." But the truth is, you do know. Everyone knows exactly what it would take to push through the impossible, and everyone has a person they would go to those lengths for. Parents never want to think about walking through the fire for their children, but they know they would. We did. We walked along the edge of the cliff and never looked at the distance to the ground or towards the clouds and sunshine. We were ready to jump at any time without a parachute should someone tell us that was the only escape route. You feel your toes gripping the edge of the mountain ready for a rockslide or earthquake at any point, but you tell yourself to not look down, to keep going. You tell yourself, "You can do this!" because you have no choice. You put one foot in front of the other, and whatever you do, you don't stop.

You learn to control your breath, because this is the one thing you can control. Slow it down and focus on this when you are overwhelmed. What an incredible tool to know about.

People would tell me, "You're so strong." Am I really? Am I that strong? Maybe. But only because I had no choice. I think I would rather be an ordinary mom, living ordinary days of mundane ordinariness, less aware of the big things and maybe even the little things, good or bad. But when you are handed a new script for your life and it does not include ordinary, you learn your lines and get on with it. There is no choice in strength or courage. They are muscles that with each invisible flex, multiply exponentially and become the backbone you rely on. The other muscles you used to enjoy using in your ordinary life slowly atrophy, and you are left with a staggering strength, kind of like The Hulk. In social situations, I would feel just like him—huge, green, so obviously different, appreciated for strength and courage with no social grace left. I can now, after much work, take the green away from my image, but I still often feel that when I'm in public and people connect me to this story, they see me for the fighter I am and no longer for the soft, ordinary girl I used to enjoy being. I hope one day to feel ordinary without losing any of this wisdom, but I know the only way to have this lens, this understanding, is to have experienced the trauma, and that's not something I can allow myself to forget. I cannot relax back into ordinary. So instead, I leap into the extraordinary and become loud and generous with my voice and decidedly steady in who I've become: the one who is not scared by childhood illness but rather feels strength and a readiness to face it.

CHAPTER 10: SMALL VICTORIES

Our reality was so goddamned painful, physically and mentally, that we quickly learned to recognize the little wins: better counts on a blood test, a bandage being removed, or finally finishing the five or six days of GCSF—granulocyte colony stimulating factor. This is a series of shots that stimulates the growth of neutrophils, a type of white blood cell important for fighting infection. I had to administer these to Nicky after every round of chemotherapy. The shot would go into his tiny thigh muscle, which was already covered in bruises from being treated like a pin cushion with very little padding. It was so traumatizing for him, and I was grateful every time we got through it.

Nicky had to be in control so we would count down from ten each time and sometimes he'd make it the first attempt, but there were days when we would need to count down from ten a dozen or more times. It was only when he said go that I was allowed to poke his tender pale skin. He would squish his eyes shut and throw his head back and finally concede, "Okay go, now!" We put little buzzing toys above the injection site or tapped somewhere else on his leg to distract from the pain and burning from the injection. It needed to be administered slowly and he would wince and whimper while trying to cooperate as best he could. I had watched the nurses administer the shots in the beginning. I think I was especially tuned into which movements worked and which didn't because I was simply more invested in preventing his tears than anyone else. When it was nearing the end of the poke (it usually took thirty to forty-five seconds as we needed to go slowly), I had to let him know so that he could brace for feeling it leave his skin. And then we were one more down and closer to our goal of good health.

These were the moments to celebrate. They were just breaks, one could argue, pauses—and that's true. They might have only been baby steps, but I felt they were moving us forward. Each one was a check in the mountain of checkboxes to get through over the course of this charade of a life. I looked for them wherever I could: the sun came out that day, our favourite nurse was on, we somewhat enjoyed a meal together, he won a game he played online against his uncles and grandfather, he could stand on his own, he could walk to the bathroom, or even just that he could walk farther than the last day. I celebrated when he put on a couple ounces of weight, when he wore clothing and not a hospital gown, when we had a day pass and could leave the hospital for a visit home for a few hours, or when we got the room we wanted within the ward. We would go for strolls through the halls of the ward in the quiet hours of the night and sometimes in the wee hours of the morning. His sweet shell of a body would move without pain for either a moment or days and I'd scream confetti in my mind as it was these moments that kept me motivated; they allowed me to see the progress he was making. It made me appreciate spending every single minute with my son and recognizing that as a gift—the gift of time.

In May, after about six rounds of chemo, Nicky came down with an infection and needed antibiotics. The problem was he hadn't gotten used to taking them in pill form yet. He had encountered so many bad tasting medicines by this time that he flat out refused the new medication. He had drawn a line in the sand, and I could not make him move. My insight let me know he felt isolated, lonely, depressed, and unrecognizable to himself. He knew I was in the same boat as him, but it was my turn to pick up the oars and row for him. Lightning struck my brain, and magic hit. I poured myself a shot of hot sauce in a medicine cup just like his. People may or may not know this about me, but spice and I do not mix. Nicky approached the table and I grinned.

"Here we go, buddy. You do yours, and I'll do mine at the same time. Let's do this." His smile and understanding that I would endure it all with him was worth every second of pain in my mouth.

Later that evening, when our second dose was due, I could have offered to drink the entire bottle of hot sauce and it wouldn't have mattered. It wasn't going to happen. Inside the house, it felt hot and stifling and his temper and panic grew worse. He was daunted by the size of the pills. We had practiced with capsule-shaped mints, and I knew he could do this. My own inner frustration flared. After an hour of begging and pleading for him to take the medication, I took the pills in one hand and his hand in the other and said, "Let's just go sit outside."

It was a beautiful, star-filled night. The cool air hit us, almost knocking us over. He looked shocked. He said it was too cold and that he wanted to go back inside. I asked him to fill his senses outside first. I wanted him to feel the cool air on his skin, to hear the sound of water trickling in our fountain, and to appreciate the beauty of the night sky. He breathed it in, closed his eyes, and paused. Then he opened his eyes and looked up at the sky. Within a few seconds, the pills were down. He woke the next morning with no pain because the antibiotics had done their job. Magic.

Darren had small victories of his own, and I could see him gaining momentum in his stride. He rallied with Clive, and he doubled down on the parenting role as "Mom-Dad" and also just Dad. When I knew in that second that I would stay with Nicky, Darren immediately committed to taking on my role in addition to his own when it came to caring for Clive. He promised to cuddle him and move him to sleep in our giant bed, so he knew he wasn't alone. He took over all the extracurricular activity planning and chauffeuring Clive's schedule entailed. He joined the WhatsApp parent group conversations for Clive's grade and began to take over all the communications and other duties that were usually my responsibility. He handled homework, playdates, checking in with the teachers, attending soccer and hockey games while running his real estate business at the same time and continuing to work out for his own stress release and sanity. He was a twelve out of ten through this for our boys. He began to sparkle in the way I knew he always could. If there is any silver lining in this awful experience, it is this. The family spotlight that usually shines on me transferred for a time to Darren, and he shone brighter than he normally would choose too. He became his best self and hit all the potential I had always seen in him. I am so grateful to know that he has this strength, this capacity to step up, and that I can count on him going forward.

He wanted to organize a new bike for Nicky. It was sweet, but the team and I knew that Nicky would not be able to use it for quite some time. Even so, I knew that this is how Darren connects with people—through action and activity. He was craving connection and struggling to find ways to feel close to Nicky. He turned to his pals, and they recommended this man named "Butter" who lived up in Squamish. During the COVID-19 pandemic, there were all kinds of supply shortages, and it was really hard to get a bike. Darren was explaining our circumstances to "Butter" and, as the discussion progressed, he found out that "Butter" was short for Butterworth. It was another serendipitous turn as this sweet gentleman was married to our surgeon, the one who had given Nicky his medcomp line. What a small world! We will always be grateful to the Butterworths for all the ways they helped us.

Even the moments that made me cringe have value. At one point, Nicky was being prepped for yet another surgery. He needed to have one of his kidney stents taken out and replaced. The other kidney stent was working well and didn't need to be touched. As we went into the waiting area for the surgery, my eyelids were sticky with exhaustion as usual, but I was alert, not because I was rested but because I had no choice. An interventional radiologist and surgeon whom I had never met before entered the room and was going over all the details of the surgery. He opened the chart he'd been given and, with certainty, began reading over it and explaining what was expected to happen. But, to my dismay, the things he said would happen were the complete opposite of what I understood were supposed to happen. I know now that he had simply been given the wrong chart of information, but in the moment, I was aghast. And I came out swinging.

"I'm sorry, but are you qualified to be working on my son?" I asked him.

Oh yeah, I said it. Not only did I stun myself with my lack of tact, but I obviously stunned him. He then laid out his qualifications and it turned out I had asked *the most qualified person in the city*. He oversaw two hospitals in his specialty. Damn! I prayed my rudeness wouldn't affect the way he worked on my boy. After everything was sorted out, the surgery went smoothly. Dr. Heron came out and apologized, saying that I should not have had to go through that and, going forward, he would be our captain when it came to Interventional Radiology. He gave me a hug and said he was sorry for what Nicky had had to go through. To this day, this man is one of our heroes and will always be a treasured friend. I am eternally grateful for his patience and kindness towards me and Nicky. We are so lucky to have met him and were blessed to have someone with his skills care for our boy. And the small victory? I learned to keep a better filter on my mouth going forward.

We got to spend my birthday at home with Nicky on a day pass. He also got to be home for Mother's Day and for Father's Day. These were important moments for us as a family, but I also interpreted them as good signs. I took them to mean that he was on the right path and things were moving the way they should be.

I learned to watch for the wins to keep my mind in a positive and hope-filled place. I'd scan the skies and move through the day looking for any clues I could use for encouragement. All the while, I monitored every detail of my child's skin and temperament in a bid to ensure success. At the end of each day, I wanted to fill him with pride about how well he'd handled whatever he'd had to face. We would finish each night with me whispering in his ear, "I love you and I'm so proud of you." Then I would have him repeat back to me "I'm proud of myself." That in itself was a victory: getting him to see his own success and his own moments of victory. It's a tradition we have kept going forward and also now extend to Clive.

CHAPTER 11: THE DIAMOND MOMENTS

My days changed from twenty-four-hour increments into a series of moments: we would share moments, and in each fragment, I would feel transcendence. I remember one such time lying next to Nicky for the first time since it all began. His body was finally stable and comfortable enough that I could sit next to him in the hospital bed. I was building him up, explaining that one day all that he has been through will be a road map for another child and that his story will shape theirs. I told him, "You'll tell them how to do it, how to get through it."

Nicky looked at me and said, without skipping a beat, "I would tell them they need my mom." My heart was struck. I will never forget that moment. It is etched into my soul and my heart for all of eternity.

I used to hold Nicky's hand as he slept; I did this so many times a day I lost count. I would hold his sweet toes and feet and give him foot rubs for hours just to bring him some reprieve. I'd hold his feet more than his hands as it seemed to disturb him less and allowed me to be close without waking him. I couldn't help myself from touching him while I had him in front of me. I never knew how long his peaceful sleep would last, and I desperately wanted to be a part of that peace he was experiencing. I also wanted to soak up as much of him as I could possibly hold in my being. I felt guilty leaving to use the bathroom because it wasn't right next to him.

But then I would lock myself in the bathroom so he couldn't see me cry as I begged any god out there to swap me in and swap him out.

My very best friend Michelle arrived at the hospital days into this chaos. We sobbed together and then sat in dumbfounded silence because there was just nothing to say. I needed her heart more than I needed my own in those early days. Hers was stronger than mine. Mine was worn out and falling apart, and she held me with steady arms. Her strength of spirit allowed me to return to Nicky's bedside with a rejuvenated spirit. Her entire family stayed steady for me and helped me to find strength for the whole journey. They are my chosen family.

My sweet fellow mama friends showed up on my birthday to give me a sweater covered in rainbow hearts so that I felt hugged while by myself in the hospital. I still wear it all the time as it reminds me that I am never alone on this road.

The school sent a care package from all the staff and students of Nicky's grade to cheer him up. It included a blanket, which he immediately wrapped himself in, and a poster signed by everyone expressing their good wishes. We taped it to the wall of the hospital room. We went through every single card that every classmate sent and allowed their words to sink in and prove to us again that we weren't alone.

Another time, in May, Nicky was home, and we had all sat down for dinner together. Between the symptoms of the disease and the side effects of the treatments and medications, Nicky had no appetite. I could see he was feeling small, low, and sad. As we sat around the table, Darren, Clive, and I ate the meal while Nicky sat quietly next to his brother, somber, dejected, and unable to overcome the taste of metals in his meal.

I paused and considered my next move. "Okay. Let's go for a drive," I said, looking at Nicky. He met my eyes, grateful for the understanding and excuse to leave the table. We left for a spin. I headed to the airport with the convertible top down and heat blasting. We went to watch the planes, something we had always loved throughout his whole childhood. I parked the car near the runways and cranked the music. I jumped out and tried to pull him out of the car to dance with me. He didn't want to. I tried hard, but I just couldn't reach his smile or find his soul. We got back into the car and headed back towards home. Then lightning struck: I had an idea. It was nearly 10:00 pm, and the skies were darkening. I headed to his school's empty parking lot. As we arrived, I put the car in park. I turned to him and tossed him the keys.

"Your turn, babe. Wanna drive?"

His eyes widened, and a disbelieving smile spread across his face. He climbed behind the wheel and buckled up. I gave him a quick explanation of the controls, and then we were off, doing circles and zigzags on the big, flat, open space, giggling all the time. Thank goodness the car was a Mini Cooper so he could reach the pedals. He then drove up the long driveway that leads to the entrance of the junior school and back down again. Then up and down again, smiling, laughing, and gaining confidence. It was such a moment of bliss. We blasted the music—Miley Cyrus, Katy Perry, and Sara Bareilles all cheered us on with uplifting songs.

The day Clive was finally allowed to visit the hospital was a big moment. I had gotten used to Facetimes with my little guy. I'd prepare prompts ahead of time—jokes, riddles, trivia—to stimulate what could sometimes be a stagnant conversation. I would download his schoolbooks to my e-reader, and we would go through his reading assignments virtually.

Clive's nickname has been Hammy since he was born. I know it wasn't easy for him to go through a pandemic as a little person: having to wear a mask, quarantine, and stay in his bubble. On top of all of this, he had to come home to an empty room that he once shared with his best friend and realize how much he missed him—and his mom. I know he felt the anxious energy within those walls every day and had to try to convince himself the situation had nothing to do with him. At the same time, he also had to try to believe he was still important and a vital component of the family.

It was such a relief to have Clive finally come to the hospital so I could show him what Nicky and I went through on a daily basis. I wanted him to understand why I needed to stay with Nicky and leave him at home. I could tell his brain hadn't let him comprehend the severity of the situation and probably wouldn't until he was well into his adulthood. I filmed the whole event. Darren met me downstairs with Clive and I ran to him. I wrapped him up in a hug and told him I had big plans for him: I was going to take him upstairs to the 8th floor and we were going to surprise Nicky. He looked at me in disbelief and, without revealing his emotions, said, "Cool," and off we went.

After we washed our hands and sanitized them before entering the ward, Melanie, Nicky's favourite nurse, met us and escorted us in. Clive had heard about her and was excited to meet her. As we entered the room, Clive hid behind the curtain as Melanie told Nicky she had a big surprise. Seeing her was one of his favourite surprises, so I could see Nicky wondering how it could get any better than that. But then Clive came around the corner and Nicky was stunned. He looked to me, then to Melanie, and then back to Clive.

"What the—? How?!" His smile stretched from ear to ear by this point and the room's energy turned gleeful. The two got comfy right away, and Clive appreciated the gaming set up the hospital had provided for Nicky.

The giggles that filled the air were heard in the hallways by the staff and other parents—they were heartwarming and healing to all those who took them in. Clive was so excited to have the chance to be there and stayed for a couple hours. The restrictions of the COVID-19 pandemic had temporarily prohibited these sibling visits for all patients in the hospital. While the goal was to protect the health of the patients and prevent the spread of the virus, these restrictions also removed a significant tool for the healing process—a vital tonic for every family's spirit. Finally getting these brothers together to share in the experience was so important and proved to be just what they needed from each other.

Getting the day pass that allowed Nicky to be the score keeper at Clive's championship Little League game was another major win. Nicky took charge of the scoreboard and his was one of the loudest cheers as Clive's team dominated and clinched the win. That night, we were invited to a beautiful housewarming party at my dear friend Allison's new home. Nicky, in an attempt to help set up the incredible spread of food, tried to open a jar of salsa. However, it slipped from his hands, and we all watched in horror as every beautiful square inch of the freshly painted surfaces was christened with a red splatter of salsa. Ally didn't miss a beat, giggling and smiling she took it in stride and told Nicky that needed to happen so that her house became a home. As we returned home that night with the top down in our Mini Cooper convertible, a supermoon had taken over Georgia Street in downtown Vancouver. It looked like a giant cookie, and I found myself imagining the Cookie Monster from Sesame Street plucking it from the sky and devouring it. I took it as a sign that things were going our way.

I was so excited to watch Nicky attend Sports Day at his school and see his friends rally around him. He was so filled with happiness. He played DJ and rolled around with Mr. Lee, the vice principal and biggest personality of the school, in the school golfcart. Every classmate wore the shirt Nicky had designed for his grade—his very own "Team Nicky" jersey. The strength of this team carried our whole family through our loneliest, darkest moments. But most of all, they carried Nicky. And that's all that mattered to me in my mind.

It was heaven to wake up in hell every day, as it meant we had one more day with our Nicky. When you are confronted with mortality, it makes you pay attention; everything else slips away into nothingness. I remember coming out of a physiotherapy appointment in May. It was for my back, which was caving in from sleeping on a cot at the hospital for so long. It was a gorgeous day—the air was fresh, and the sun was shining. I looked around stunned as I exited the building because I didn't recognize the season. There were flowers on the trees and in the gardens. How did that happen? It was like we skipped spring. When we had entered the hospital there had been snow on the ground. Now everything was green and there was warmth in the sun. I realized I hadn't looked up once. Not once.

If I have learned anything from this experience, it is the importance of staying present—*in the moment*. That was the secret for me. When Nicky was diagnosed, we were all robbed of the future in an instant: robbed of his dreams for himself, of our dreams for him, of our dreams for our family as a whole. Even looking to the next season and the change in the weather seemed uncertain. When robbed of tomorrow, the only option for survival is to stay in today, and sometimes in the hour, and sometimes in the minute.

CHAPTER 12: SELF CARE: MENTAL AND PHYSICAL

How do you take care of yourself mentally and physically when you are the caregiver? It's hard, and it really never feels as though you have any reprieve. The trauma of your suffering as you watch your child struggle through illness is overwhelming. Yet it doesn't compare to the actual pain of what your child is experiencing so you have to maintain a quiet, solemn calm through the chaos.

No matter what I was feeling, I would lie on my cot in the hospital and be as steady as possible so as not to spread weakness to Nicky. I needed him to know that I was strong in all areas of my life. He had to feel my certainty that we had this. There was no room for one negative moment of fear.

So, how did I manage this? Reiki.

I used to think Reiki was an alternative practice that wouldn't help me through anything—or would it? Cindy and I met a few weeks after Nicky was first admitted to the hospital. A close friend whom I respect greatly had referred her and her services to me. Cindy is an intuitive coach, medium, and Reiki master. As it turns out, she and I had grown up blocks from each other and had been friends with girls who were from the same family. Cindy had been friends with Sara, and I had grown up with her younger sister, Cecilia. We figured out we had even hung out at their house at the same time—another lightning strike!

At first, I wasn't sure Reiki would be something I would enjoy, but it turned out to be exactly the grounding I needed at that moment. In the weeks following Nicky's diagnosis, I felt like I had been tied to the back of a car and was being pulled through the mud. The world looked murky and slow to me. Enter Cindy. Initially, she offered to help me with a remote Reiki session. I agreed because, well, she offered, and I was curious to try it and see what it might do for me.

As the session began, I sat cross-legged and closed my eyes, preparing for I don't know what. I took a few deep breaths and then with a crash of energy, a wave of purple filled my closed eyes and my body felt heavy. I couldn't believe I was feeling such strong pulses of energy. I'd never felt anything like it in my life. Wave after wave of flowing energy rippled through my body. It felt like a weighted gravity streamed through the top of my head into my skull and down through my body. Behind my closed eyes, I saw dark shades of indigo and purple, almost like ink spreading through water, or smoke filling the air. As the session concluded, I was convinced I should continue my practice of Reiki with Cindy. A friendship and trust formed between us, and I knew I had found someone incredible I could count on for honest moments.

Eventually Nicky grew curious and asked to try it. We complied and when he said didn't feel anything, Cindy told me that she saw a man holding a lightning bolt floating above Nick. He asked to try again and this time he felt it; he explained that it was like he was floating above his body and that all the pain was below him. That was all Cindy and I needed to hear. Cindy continued to lead Reiki sessions with Nicky regularly, any time he'd request it: before, after, sometimes even *during* his procedures. Can

I prove that it works? Not physically. But mentally, it brought us a calm we had been missing as we dealt with this illness and the treatment. If nothing else, it provided me with a reason to focus on our minds, uninterrupted, for twenty minutes or so. The quiet meditative state it creates is so restorative I have continued on with it. I'd encourage people to be open and to look outside the box when it comes to the needs you don't even know you have—until you do.

Three years down the road, Cindy and I are still very close. Her friendship and guidance have helped me to grow and heal, and I am so grateful to have her in my life. Our relationship is profound and moving and deep. She was the first person I called to share my joy at learning that Nicky had clear scans. I love her for what she has brought to my world and mostly for who she is. She helped carry me through my darkest days.

Pet therapy also played a significant role in helping us keep it together. Early on, one of our doctors organized a visit from a therapy dog—a golden Labrador named Gaia. Gaia usually works at Vancouver's Children's Hospice, Canuck Place, with Dr. Natasha Datoo, but after pulling some strings, Dr. Natasha was able to get permission for her to make a special visit just for Nicky. I had wondered why Dr. Natasha got involved with us from the beginning and, looking back, I wonder if it was because of the severity of Nicky's illness and the possibility that he might eventually end up in hospice care. It's a chilling reminder of how it could have gone either way. Regardless, I am so grateful to Dr. Natasha for bringing that doggo in for us. The moment Gaia came into the room with her tail wagging and hopped up on the bed and cuddled with Nicky, everything was suddenly better. Gaia was able to comfort him without judgement as he found solace in her soft, fluffy fur and her gentle, brown eyes. I wonder if this pup knows how important her job is. Sparky, our own little rescue pup, would take over the reins whenever we were able to return home. Otherwise, Sparky would often make trips to the entrance of the hospital where he would sit so still on Nicky's lap so Nicky could cuddle him. He was always so gentle. He never flinched or got spooked despite all the medical equipment, tubes, and wires.

The comfort these animals brought was needed beyond words. This was the kindness Nicky craved. It calmed his anxiety tremendously. There is something magical about dogs and pet therapy. I believe that there are angels on this earth to watch over us; some have wings and others have four paws and fur. We need both to get through the hardest times.

CHAPTER 13: THE WHALE

It was the middle of August 2021, and we were at our cabin in Parksville, BC. Darren and I had been arguing about I-don't-remember-what, and I felt so alone. I wiped the tears off my cheeks and grabbed a kayak. Moving swiftly so no one could pull me back inside with another demand, I paddled quickly and efficiently to escape into the deep parts of the water. Once I had reached my boundary for depth and distance, I stopped and breathed in deeply. I breathed again and again. Hot tears slid down my cheeks. I tried to find my breath, tried to control it. Feeling the kid-sized craft sway with the gentle waves underneath me, I finally began to relax. The tension slowly melted out of my shoulders and back, and I felt water dripping down my leg from the paddle. I remembered thinking, "No one can get to me here. They can't hear me, and I can't hear them."

But then I heard it: "PSHHHHHHHH!" I froze scanning the water. A minute later, it happened again. "PSHHHHHHHH!!" I realized I was hearing whales coming up for air somewhere close by, but I couldn't see them. Where were they? I could hear them, breath after breath, for a long while. I relaxed into the moment and took it in. I was in absolute awe. I wasn't sure why I'd been blessed to experience this moment, but I felt more connected to the universe than I had in a long while, and I didn't feel so alone anymore. The breathing noises eventually ceased, but I continued to stay silent and still for an hour. I returned to shore, tucking the memory into my soul for safe keeping. I was grateful.

A week or so later, we returned home to Vancouver and were at the hospital having a meeting to discuss possible outcomes of a complex surgery Nicky was going to have to undergo as part of his treatment. I have to preface this with a reminder of how much I disliked the big meetings and how much they overwhelmed me. The medical team began with a description of the procedure: they were planning to cut across his abdomen and try to remove everything that was near his bowel and large intestine as well as a couple of lymph nodes. There were many risks to the procedure, one being Nicky needing an ostomy bag after the procedure. This is a medical device that is attached externally to the intestine to bypass an internal part of the intestine that is injured or not working correctly. It gathers waste produced by the body and is emptied by the patient daily. The question was, should we let Nicky know of this risk ahead of time or not worry him and just deal with it if and when it became a reality. That commitment to him to never lie hung over my heart. This was the ultimate trigger for me.

Nearly twenty years before, an important person in my life had battled colitis. His bowel was leaking into his body, and he was near death; he had four hours to make a life-or-death decision. It was either attach the bag, or he would lose his life. Everything had been done to prevent or avoid this complication, but it was no use. As I looked at my person, he resolved to attach the bag. The moment he agreed, I rallied behind him and got on board. We had no choice and just had to accept this. After a grueling, thirteen-hour surgery, my person awoke with a scar that ran vertically around his belly button and went downwards for something like thirty staples. This person healed and then had to undergo another very long operation to reattach his intestine to his body nearly a year later. Luckily, he was able to stop using the ostomy bag and is alive and thriving but knowing that my son could wake to this same fate stole the air from lungs. It was happening again. I couldn't catch my breath. Damn!

The tears spilled from my eyes. I had really wanted to appear composed in this meeting with Dr. Rod and Dr. Webber, our incredible general surgeon. I looked out the window in an attempt to hide the truth of my emotions, but they were filling my eyes and streaming down my cheeks. As I sat in shock, my thoughts heavy with haze, suddenly I heard it:

"PSHHHHHHH!"

I actually heard the whale breathe! And I could see it breach in my mind. "Breathe," I told myself. "Just breathe. Slowly, in and out. Deep breaths. You can't control this situation, but you can control your breath."

Gradually, I started to comprehend. Now I understood why I had heard them, and not seen them as I had hoped to. Because in moments of chaos, you cannot always see clearly. Instead, you need to trust your breath and focus on it to push through the waves to steady ground. So, as a team we pushed through together, my whales and me.

After the procedure, Nicky woke to a couple tubes he hadn't known about and was startled and frustrated because of the unexpected inconvenience of them and the feeling they caused. Due to the medication, he grew angry and agitated with both Darren and me. Darren was alarmed. He had never encountered this aspect of the hospital stay or this side of Nicky. I had sheltered him from the storm deliberately as I knew it wasn't where he wanted to be. I could see Darren cracking wide open there—feeling helpless and wanting so badly to make it better. Suddenly he understood what I had been keeping from him. It was written in the sweat on his forehead and the crease between his brows. He was feeling it all in one evening. He was catching up to where I had been all along.

The evening passed and Nicky woke the next day with an epidural, and he felt pretty good. It turned out the cut had not been the one we anticipated, which would run from hip bone to hip bone horizontally. His scar ran vertically around his belly button and down his torso. In fact, he had the exact scar as my person, without having the need of an ostomy bag. They matched and I knew in that instant that we had a homerun. Lightning!

I'm so sorry my person had to endure what they went through, but in hindsight, I am so grateful that they were willing to allow me to walk along the road with them. It helped this moment in Nicky's cancer treatment journey feel a little familiar and, in retrospect, it helped me to feel a bit safer.

This person gave me the following quote, and it's as true today as it was in those moments.

> *I don't want to die without any scars. They're the proof that we lived with passion and purpose. A scar is a tattoo from life itself.*
> —Chuck Palahniuk

CHAPTER 14: COVID

September 2021 began with a bang. Nicky was scheduled for his final round of chemo before his stem cell transplant and Clive was about to start his new school: an all-boys prep school where the majority of his preschool pals had gone directly from kindergarten. Everything seemed to be aligning, except Darren and I were at our breaking point again. We were not connecting—we weren't communicating effectively and there was no understanding between us as to the fact that the way we dealt with and digested our situation was different. A giant pile of resentment was building.

My husband had planned to go on a boys' trip to Vegas with his friends. I couldn't understand it. The COVID-19 pandemic was very much still in our midst, and Darren wasn't the best at masking or hand sanitizing. As luck would have it, the day before Darren was to leave, we got a notice from Clive's school that we would have to homeschool him as so many of his fellow students had tested positive for the virus. Clive didn't have any symptoms, but just to be safe, we arranged for him to take an antigen test. Darren was taking the same kind of test before his trip. They both came back negative, and we felt instant relief. Darren planned to go ahead with his trip.

When I mentioned the situation at Clive's school to our GP, he voiced concerned for Nicky, who was immunocompromised and fragile from his illness. He told me we needed to be extra careful to protect him from being exposed to the virus and recommended we schedule the more sensitive PCR test for Clive. So, we did—and he tested positive. My poor Clive was terrified. He was only eight years old, and he had been learning about COVID-19 like the rest of us—through the news headlines. There was so much uncertainty and worry about the virus. We were all panicking, but poor Clive wasn't sure if the worry was for him or for his brother. He looked like he was scared he had done something bad. I assured him that it wouldn't matter what germ he had, we were going to take care of him. Nicky would be fine, and so would he.

I was going to need help, though. There was a chance Clive had exposed all of us to the virus, but the only way forward that I could see was for me to stay with Nicky and use all the recommended safety protocols while taking care of him to ensure that I wouldn't pass it to him. I asked Darren to take Clive to a hotel or to our cabin in Parksville to keep him away from Nicky. Darren looked me square in the eye and flat out refused. He said he had committed to the trip to Vegas, but I knew his fellow travelers would completely understand that he had to bow out given the circumstances. I was dumbfounded.

"But you committed to our family first. You are a member of our family. We need you," I pleaded. "This isn't even normal circumstances; we have an immunocompromised child that we're trying to protect, and a young boy who is terrified of the virus and what it will do to him and his brother and family. *This* is the priority!"

But Darren refused again. I was stunned. As he grabbed his bag and went to meet the taxi, I looked at him and knew this was the limit for us. He was crossing a line. I lost it. I spewed names as the tears fell and begged him to stay. In one last attempt, I asked him to admit that he was behaving like a selfish prick. With one hand on the door to the taxi, he turned, suitcase in hand, and looked right at me.

"Yep, I'm being a selfish prick," he said.

The satisfaction I thought I would feel from that admission never came. I was just hurt, and the sense of abandonment crept in and solidified. He'd left me when I needed him the most—when *we* needed him the most—again.

It was down to me. I called my friend Dana and told her what had happened. Dana is the mother of Clive's very best friend Cole and two other boys. As I was relating my tale of woe to her, she told me that all three of her kids had tested positive for COVID! She swooped in and saved me, volunteering to take Clive in at her house. She told me to check with the local health authority to be sure we could do what she suggested. Once we had, within an hour Clive had been packed up and picked up and was being made to feel like a guest of honour at Dana's place. She took on the homeschooling duties, snuggled him, and made sure he felt loved; as for Clive, he played and partied in his pajamas with his best mates!

For me, the guilt I felt about this whole situation was almost too much to bear, even though I knew it was the only way. Still, I hated not being the one to care for my youngest child, especially when I knew he already felt slighted because of our circumstances. It was a miserable time. Nicky and I wore masks, and I spent every spare moment meticulously cleaning surfaces with antibacterial wipes and swabs. I cuddled my sweet boy's feet so that we could feel close—but from a safe distance. I was on fumes and ready to put it to a vote if Darren should remain on the island.

Darren eventually returned and took Clive to Parksville and relaxed with him over there while I kept up the new hygiene standards at home. Nicky never tested positive, and he remained safe thanks to our friends, Dana and her husband, Eric. They didn't have to help, but they did. I have no idea how I will ever repay them as they literally picked me up at my worst moment and held me together. I may have been let down badly at home, but I have never felt so safe and cared for by my friends and community as I did that week.

CHAPTER 15: CAN YOUR RELATIONSHIP SURVIVE THE FIRE?

Throughout Nicky's illness and treatment, my relationship with Darren ebbed and flowed not so gracefully. Essentially, we lived separately for the better part of a year and to be honest, it worked for us. I stayed with Nicky, and he stayed with Clive. All the while, I kept fantasizing that this would bring us back on the same page. I think he hoped the same. But in reality, it spread us further apart. He learned that I am far more capable and self-sufficient than he—or I—ever gave me credit for. I proved that I can hold my children through hell and ensure they come out on the other side with less harm than anticipated.

I have spent so much of our marriage feeling lonely and isolated. I felt that if I disappeared, I'd only be missed because there would be no one to look after the kids or make dinner. It's not a nice way to go to sleep at night. We had been attending couples therapy with a few different professionals before Nicky's diagnosis; however, it always ended with Darren eventually refusing to attend and me continuing with the therapist alone.

He would tell me he didn't need or want to change his way of life. His priority was socializing with his friends. All that mattered was that he was constantly invited to the party; I guess those experiences helped his self-esteem. Regardless, my needs always took a backseat.

Darren's upbringing was safe and uneventful except for his parents' dynamic with each other and his father's attitude towards women in general. His dad, a white man who grew up in the 1960s with three siblings, was raised by a single mother. As an adult he was used to working hard and getting his way. Darren's mother—a woman I have always looked up to as both beautiful and intelligent—was raised to keep silent. I recall her explaining to me when my marriage was still very new, that her childhood with immigrant parents from India was marked by her family's belief that women should have no voice—that, by virtue of being a girl, she held no value. Being raised in this atmosphere of chauvinism made an impact on Darren and his siblings. This was when they learned that being honest about their vulnerability would only hurt them in the end. This was when they were taught never to share who they really are and never to appear weak. It's understandable that Darren would never discuss hard things. Hard things weren't discussed in his home when he was growing up, and he wasn't shown how to communicate and move through to resolve things with heart. If he wasn't taught these things or that men can show up in all kinds of ways for their partners, how was Darren to know how to discuss anything or show up for me? It took Nicky being diagnosed with cancer for Darren to even broach the topic of cancer with his own dad—and his dad had been diagnosed with cancer twenty years before!

From my side, my own family never resolved anything without temper tantrums and yelling. Guilt was always part of the conversation. My mother battled depression and struggled with mental health issues all her life. My dad believed as long as he provided the necessities, and maybe even some luxuries, he was a good dad. Both my mom and dad were from broken homes and moved often as children—changing neighbourhoods and schools. So, they wanted to give their kids more stability. That meant one home they could always return to. They are still in that home. Neither of them wanted their children to experience divorce, so they were determined to stay together.

In retrospect, I think that adherence to their commitment might have been as toxic as a broken home. Neither of them had been provided with an example of a successful relationship, so they couldn't pass down to their three kids the tools required to effectively and calmly communicate in relationships. I remember dating a boy in high school and having to allow him to read my diary because I could not articulate my own feelings. I learned early on that my mom's feelings were far more important than my own. How her day went was more important than how mine did. I never learned how to feel my own feelings until I began to work on this with good teachers, counsellors, and therapists and by reading certain authors and listening to speakers who were experts on the subject. I would absorb the dominant energy in the room and silence my own. I needed to retrain my brain—rewire it actually—to improve my relationships.

This all sounds pretty bad, but I want to make clear that I know both our families did the best they could with the tools they had. No one is perfect, and I am certainly no exception. They loved their kids the best way they knew how but neither situation was ideal, and the struggles Darren and I faced in our relationship were inevitable and real.

I knew who I married, and he was still that fun, party guy. He made everyone around him feel included and important. Everyone except me. I was just supposed to be grateful for everything he provided, but it's not about things for me. I wanted more from his spirit. He is a caring father, but somehow our relationship—our marriage—had become the collateral damage in his bid to maintain his party lifestyle. He would always be travelling on boys' trips and going to big dinners out, inevitably returning boozy. I felt forgotten, no longer special. I would retreat deeper and deeper into myself, confused about what I had done to deserve this abandonment. As I worked with counsellors and began to study tools for relationships and psychology within relationships, I began to build back some of the confidence I had lost—and even gained a speck of gumption.

Finally, at the end of 2019, after speaking with some trusted friends, I took charge and met with several well-known and respected lawyers. My heart had already been broken by Darren's choices, but I thought the best thing for my children would be for them to see me put myself first for once; however, over the course of Nicky's illness, I reconsidered, and Darren and I both took steps that helped us arrive at a meeting of the minds. We agreed the kids had to be put first—full stop. We agreed we had to learn to respect each other and, having just met with lawyers and experienced some not so nice interactions, we realized we had to build from zero again. It felt foreign to both of us. We had both grown so bitter and independent. Over the course of nearly an entire year, we slept together in the same bed maybe five times. So, there just wasn't any opportunity during that period to rebuild anything romantic. Instead, we were forced to become allies, a dependable force for each other.

A major turning point in our relationship had actually occurred in February 2020, over a year before Nicky's diagnosis. We had decided to sell a property and each and every time we did this in our life together, Darren would always insist that his sister Leslie be our realtor, and that we would pay her a discounted rate. It was really hard to watch as she is a very accomplished realtor in her industry; but, because she sold houses and not industrial buildings like the men in the family, she was deemed less worthy. The inherent disrespect in expecting her to essentially donate her professional services always bothered me, but this time it struck a chord. I realized it was yet another case of a woman's work being taken for granted, and I just couldn't let it happen again.

This time, before she agreed to represent us and the agreement was signed, I demanded she be paid her full commission. For the first time ever, I took a stand and put my foot down. From that moment on, I found my voice, and with it, my backbone. I really believe this was the difference for Darren and me. By standing up for his sister and insisting he respect her professional skills, I think I won something important for myself: Darren's respect. Plus, the fact of the matter is, she is a leader in her industry, a true professional and a talented realtor—perhaps the best in her family. And she had our back throughout this chaos. She and her own family provided a soft place where Nicky felt safe enough to be himself. When we would share a meal, Nicky never felt like he had to wear a hat to cover his sweet bald head. He never felt he had to temper his conversations to make them feel comfortable. Around his Auntie Leslie, her partner's family, and his cousins he felt accepted and supported. He was still just Nicky.

Darren's behaviour when Clive got COVID is hard to understand. But, in hindsight, I see that it was a reaction to an untenable situation. I know now that Darren had reached his breaking point, and he needed to exit quickly. Do I wish he'd handled it differently? Do I wish he'd been able to talk to me about how he felt? Of course. But I know that he didn't have the tools to process his feelings in a healthy way. I can understand that, and while it hurt in the moment, when I think back on that event, I now view it with more compassion. We have never spoken about that time. Maybe we will in therapy one day. Maybe we won't. Either way, I forgive him.

CHAPTER 16: PARADE DAY —OUR D DAY

By the fall of 2021, we were almost at the end of Nicky's thirteen rounds of chemotherapy. It had been such a punishing road. The treatments left Nicky exhausted and nauseated and he became increasingly anxious about them. It was getting harder and harder to get him to the hospital for them. I knew this was going to be the toughest round yet. For this final round, Nicky would have to endure a higher dose of chemo and then would have to be isolated for at least a month as he underwent his stem cell treatment.

We all knew this was coming, including Nicky. It was going to be a major struggle to get him out of bed and into the car, so I asked a core group of women to help me plan something so epic that it would bleed hope and inspire courage. I had a vision of a highway with people cheering on the sides. Similar to the highway of tears for fallen soldiers, this would be a highway of hope to help a child overcome the impossible in his mind. When I called my close friend Paula and explained what I had hoped to plan for Nicky, she said, "I've got this. I'll take it from here." And, oh my goodness, did she ever! What she and our friends planned took hold in the community and snowballed into a legendary event.

On October 12th, I woke up early and while Nicky still slept, I had an interview with the local news team to share my plan. The community had organized a surprise that would be remembered in our city for generations! People were going to come out and cheer Nicky on as he made his way to the hospital this morning. Dozens, maybe hundreds of our friends were going to be lining the sidewalks to support him. Somehow, I had managed to keep it a secret from both Nicky and Clive. After one more bid to get the information out publicly via the interview, I made my way to his room and began psyching myself up—it was going to take a lot of convincing just to get him to the car.

I grabbed my prop and tucked it deep in my pocket.

As I entered the room, I saw Nicky was curled up in his pajamas—*The Flash* themed obviously—and was snuggling with our dog, Sparky. I prayed for him and the universe to forgive me for waking him up. I touched his shoulder gently and kissed his sweet cheek. "Nicky? Time to get up, love."

He replied with a hearty, "Hell no! You can't make me. I'm not going."

I nodded in agreement and said, "Yeah, I figured as much . . . well how about we forget what's supposed to happen this afternoon and instead see if we can manage the morning?"

"You're NOT going to manage me today, Mom. You can't make me go!"

"I'm not even talking about the hospital, babe. I have something else planned that will blow your mind," I said cryptically, trying to tempt him.

"No, you don't. And it wouldn't matter if you did. I don't care," he spat back.

Taking a deep breath, I steadied myself. "Here we go," I thought. I reached for my prop and put it down next to him on the pillow. "I just thought we could begin the day with a beautiful drive."

He shook his head adamantly and then paused slightly as he glanced at the car key I had placed near his hand.

"Are you sure, bud? It's such a nice car . . ."

"What key is that? What car? You know what? It doesn't matter anyway. I'm not going," he said.

"Okay, well if you're even just a little bit interested, maybe we could just go downstairs and take a peek at the car. It's in the garage." I picked up the key and began to walk towards the door. "I promise you I won't force you to do anything. I keep my promises, Nicky. Just come and see it."

I could see that curiosity was getting the better of him. So, I tossed him a pair of track pants and his favourite hoodie. "It's cold outside, just put these on. I'll go in front of you and keep my hands in my pockets so I can't make you do anything. Promise."

He hesitated but then conceded and got dressed. We walked to the garage and opened the door. Inside was *the* most beautiful, shiny, fire-engine red Ferrari waiting to take him on the adventure. His jaw dropped and his face froze. I knew it was working! He looked at me in absolute confusion and wonder.

"Nicky, since it's here, wouldn't it be a shame not to at least hear the growl of the engine? How about it? Do you wanna hear it?" I asked.

He nodded, still in shock. I opened the door, got in the driver's seat, and turned the car on so it could growl for my boy. Lightning flashed across his eyes. I could see his excitement. I knew I'd almost got him. "Come on, magic!" I prayed.

"How about we don't think about this afternoon, and we take this baby for a little drive? What do you think, Nicky?"

Still speechless, he opened the passenger door and sat on the tan leather interior. Seat belts, music, growls from the engine, and then we were off. We took a spin around the neighbourhood and then headed straight over to Clive's school. Until this morning, Clive didn't know about the surprise. I didn't want him to feel the weight of keeping such a big secret for too long, and I really wanted him to enjoy the craziness of this wild day too.

Nicky was sitting back now, but I could tell he didn't quite trust me yet.

I told him, "This morning is just about us; there is no agenda. I just want us to enjoy the day and each other."

He smiled pensively as I zigzagged through the neighbourhood in a car that's not meant to be swirling around those streets. I made my turn and landed on the street with our first stop—Clive's school. It's a beautiful, old castle-like building and has a circular driveway that usually is not open to the public. But today, the gates were wide open, and lining the drive were Clive's grade 4 class and what would be Nick's grade 7 class, all with signs and cheering loudly for Nicky and Clive. I froze. It was so much to take in. Even though we'd planned it, I was still amazed as I saw it happening in front of me.

As Nicky and I drove along in the Ferrari, my Mini Cooper convertible appeared behind us with Darren at the wheel and my brother Ryan in the backseat. We passed by Clive, standing alongside his friends and cheering for Nicky. A shy smile had spread across Nicky's face as he took it all in, enjoying the moment. Clive's friends embraced him, and the teachers told him to get in the car with his dad. He looked at them in disbelief and later told me he couldn't believe that he was getting to leave because he had a big test that day. His eyes were wide, and he was smiling excitedly. I was praying that he too would feel special. I gave Darren the signal, and Nicky and I turned right while Darren, Clive, and Ryan turned left.

Nicky looked at me nervously and asked suspiciously, "Where are we going?"

"Why don't we get on a road where we can really open this baby up?" I responded. He smiled and nodded and off we went to find the highway near our neighbourhood. I floored it and allowed him to feel some speed. I told him to harness that speed in his mind. The two of us giggled and laughed and played on that road with so much glee and happiness.

While Nicky and I had a joyride in the Ferrari, Clive returned home with Darren and Uncle Ryan to pick up Auntie Lisa and Kevin Gordon. Through his organization, The Driven Project, Kevin has curated a network of drivers and supercars to help create special experiences and memories for kids battling life-threatening illnesses. I was initially hesitant to reach out to him as I felt guilty; I wasn't sure we were eligible for inclusion in his program. But he was so welcoming and as he described what it could be like for us to participate, my excitement grew. I was humbled by his genuine kindness. He and his team are first class and will forever be a part of our history.

When Clive, Darren, and Uncle Ryan arrived, they found a turquoise Lamborghini parked in front of our house. Kevin was waiting out front to tell Clive that he was going to get to ride in the supercar. I can only imagine Clive's reaction. Darren said his jaw dropped.

"Holy what?!" exclaimed Clive. From the time he was two years old and able to point and convey his opinion, Clive has consistently pointed out Lamborghinis and claimed them as *his* car. I knew this would be a dream come true for him.

As Nicky and I neared the end of the long, open road, we approached the next stop of the parade. I sent out a warning text and continued driving. We began the ascent of the hill towards Nicky's school. At this point, he was calling me out. "Mom, I'm on to you." But was he really? He had no idea.

As we turned the corner, we saw that the entire school was out and lining the street. There were hundreds of students and teachers. Banners and flags waved, and everyone screamed at the top of their lungs. Journalists with news cameras approached the car as we drove by slowly, and they began to interview Nicky paparazzi style.[3]

"How you doing, Nicky?"

"I'm good, thanks," he answered, grinning nervously. His worries melted away, and the Nicky that enjoyed magic appeared. His eyes sparkled and his smile was infectious.

"What do you think of this crowd?"

"This is amazing!" he exclaimed.

His classmates started calling him The Fresh Prince of the West Side, acknowledging that turnouts like this only happen for celebrities like Harry Styles or Barack Obama. They joined the journalists and started to engage with Nicky to let him know they believed in him.

"You are so strong, and we are so proud of you. You're just so amazing," said classmate and friend Addison Jones as the news cameras rolled. "We all look up to you and you can do this. We got you!"

Nicky got out of the car and began waving like a seasoned superstar to the adoring crowds. He crossed the street to high five his friends and hug his grandmother and cousins who had also arrived. Clive and Darren appeared on the sidewalk and took in the epic chaos of love—it echoed in all our ears.

When the camera crews approached me for comment, I said, "He is so loved. And it's just people having the opportunity to show up. If you give

3 For the news story, see: https://bc.ctvnews.ca/rockstar-sendoff-for-b-c-12-year-old-on-way-to-final-chemo-appointment-1.5620492

people the opportunity, I believe in the good and magic of the world and this is what comes of it." Looking around in that moment, I knew what I had said was true. It's allowing people in on those hard days and in those dark moments. It's not just about asking for help. It's also about taking it all in when it does show up.

Darren was also interviewed. He said, "Nobody imagined it would snowball like it did. It went viral and it's mind-blowing. It's overwhelming. It's incredible." He sounded so eloquent when he spoke, but I saw it. Darren was having a hard time keeping his voice from cracking and his eyes from leaking all the gratitude and grief that he was feeling. It's really one of the few times that he wasn't able to hide it from me. It's a beautiful thing when people let you see them.

Nicky wandered over to the Lamborghini.

"Hi Nicky! What do you think? You wanna start this thing up?" asked Kevin.

"Sure!"

"Great. I think you should. Come here."

With encouragement from his new friend Kevin and his supercar friends, Nicky got into the seat of the Lamborghini. Kevin showed him how to push the accelerator and they listened to the purr of a real engine. He pointed out all the features and explained everything about the car. Nicky, grinning and giggling, was overwhelmed; his head spun with dreams of driving a car like that one day. He revved the engine, and his classmates went wild. I could see Nicky's heart soar. The cars were absolutely breathtaking, and we stored the torque we felt in them for later when we would need some extra energy to get through the hard times. Kevin will have our gratitude forever.

"Nicky! Nicky! Nicky!" The cries repeated over and over and filled the air. Signs bobbed along in unison with lightning bolts etched in bright colours on posterboards. Nicky exited the Lamborghini and waved to the crowd like a champion. Kevin encouraged the cheers to get louder.

"N! I! C! K! N! I! C! K!" The crowd shouted, spelling out his name.

Nicky and Clive's cousins Lily and Marcus got into the supercars for the big ride, and Clive retook his spot in the turquoise Lamborghini. Then the Vancouver Police Department arrived. I expected one or two officers, but what showed up was a procession fit for a king. Motorcycles and squad cars with full lights blazing came to escort our parade of hope and courage along the route to BCCH.

As we drove along, we passed friends with local businesses standing on the corners holding signs and screaming at the top of their lungs. All down the road we saw signs with lightning bolts emblazoned with "You've got this!" and "GO NICKY GO!" Gradually, we began our ascent into the calm, residential streets of the West Side of Vancouver. On every corner, friends, classmates, neighbours—and even strangers—held signs and jumped with joy sending us all the courage they could muster. Nicky and I could feel it all. For me, it felt downright spiritual. I tried to take in every face that I saw, make eye contact, wave, and say thank you, but I know I missed people along the way. I hope they know how eternally grateful my family will be to each and every person who stood alongside us, making sure we knew we were not alone in this fight for our child's life.

We passed another neighbourhood elementary school and saw all these kids, none of whom we knew, had made signs and were screaming louder than the last corner of people. They didn't even know my child, and yet, here they were.

We reached a main intersection, rounded the corner, and gasped. More and more people just kept appearing! How did we know so many people? A friend who literally had had a baby that week was standing there holding her newborn and cheering with her husband. Dads of Nicky and Clive's classmates had dressed up with wigs and yellow cheer gear to encourage Nicky along the way, and no doubt to show Darren they understood what it meant to be a dad. All the moms who had helped me organize this were there too. I saw each and every one, and I know Nicky did too. The younger children of our friends, who now attended the same preschool that our kids had attended long ago, also lined the street. Even our radiologist's child was there. The staff from our club, where our kids swim and play sports, came out on the corner and cheered and kids from yet another two schools lined the streets.

Friends who I hadn't spoken to in ages made eye contact with me and in that split second, we caught up to where we were, and I felt every bit of love that I had forgotten was there. Sometimes love is invisible. Sometimes love can't show up the way you think it should or need it to, but that doesn't mean it's not there. Sometimes the invisible love is the strongest and the moment it reveals itself to you, it repairs more of your heart than you thought needed fixing to begin with.

Our entourage approached the main intersection of King Edward Avenue and Granville Street. By now, the procession was so huge, I wondered how we would all cross together. The answer blew my mind. The police motorcycles went ahead and flashed their lights to signal the police cars and their dog squad that was already there and waiting to stop traffic. They saluted Nicky and me as we passed. I have no words for how moving this was. Perfect strangers, who were now stuck in traffic, waved and cheered, smiling and clapping. They didn't even know who we were. I tucked the encouragement of those people into my heart for safekeeping. I still look to it on hard days.

We rounded Oak Street, the next main intersection, and again the police stopped traffic. We saw Darren's work colleagues on the corner. There were also women who used to babysit Nicky when he was a toddler, as well as women who were working through their own grief because cancer had struck their family. They all stood in solidarity with each other, and my heart caught in my throat. We were getting closer to the hospital. I glanced at Nicky. His smile was still ear to ear. Relief flooded my heart—the plan was working.

The Vancouver Canucks hockey team mascot, an irrepressible Orca whale named Fin, waited at the entrance of the hospital, ready to shower Nicky with gifts. As we got closer, we encountered a mob of close family and friends. My parents were there, front and centre, as were my brothers and their children. Nicky's absolute best friends in the world, the hair cut crew, all showed up. Our oncologist was also there and explained to more camera crews that he had never seen a hospital admission or stay with an entrance like this. My brothers charged Nicky and hugged him fiercely as he was presented with more certifications and gifts from the Vancouver Police Department cycling team, a charity that supports the fight against cancer.

As the hugs and pictures continued, a clock ticked in the back of my mind. I knew that as much as this was the greatest idea I had ever come up with, what goes up must come down, and I feared the fall from this height would be extra painful. I pushed the worry away. I wanted to focus on the excitement and enjoy watching Nicky be happy and carefree for just a little longer. But the hugs did end eventually. Kevin and his crew wished us good luck and promised Nicky that they would be his official chauffeurs any time he needed them. His best mates, Ryan, Austin, Imran, Matthew, Laughlin, and Clive clung to the remaining moments together, promising Nicky that they would see him online and would keep in touch via Facetime.

Clive soaked up as much as he could from me and from the excitement. I promised him in a whisper that I would make it up to him. I saw Dr. Rod slowly begin to pick up the packages and gifts and start to head to the door. I hugged my baby brother and his wife Lisa, holding them close.

They gave me the soft love I needed. I went to my brother Jason and his wife Luisa—my rocks—and with their reassuring nods, got the strength to walk inside. We gave everyone one final wave and they gave us one last cheer. We entered like heroes.

"We've got this," I said. And we did.

As heart-warming and encouraging as the parade was, it still couldn't change one unfortunate aspect: timing. We entered the hospital on October 12th, just five days before Clive's birthday. Clive had to celebrate his big day in the hospital, sacrificing his hope to finally be the centre of attention at a fun-filled celebration for him; he had to share the spotlight with Nicky yet again. We did our best to focus on him: we decorated the room as best we could, and we brought in a fancy birthday cake and the best birthday presents. Still, it felt sterile. Nicky attended the birthday for as long as he could, but he had received his chemo and was beginning to feel nauseated and fatigued. He tired quickly and had to return to his room to rest.

I kissed Clive so many times that day. I snuggled him so hard. I knew we were fast approaching the isolation period and I would have to forfeit those touches for a while. Having to leave one child to care for the other was awful. As I kissed him, I knew that the next time I'd see him would be on a Zoom call. This was my last chance to smell his hair, touch his smooth skin, and kiss his perfect cheekbones. I swallowed my tears.

I will never get those moments with Clive back, and I will never stop making it up to him. I pray that he understands why I had to do what I did and be where I needed to be. I also hope he doesn't hold onto any anger. We both felt the anguish of our separation equally. Clive was never my second choice. He and Nicky will forever be equal in my heart. Always.

CHAPTER 17: STEM CELL TRANSPLANT

After he received the final, high dose of chemotherapy, Nicky's cells were expected to stop regenerating. This is how the doctors planned to wipe out all the cancerous cells. He would need a stem cell transplant after the chemotherapy to replenish his body with healthy new cells that would be able to reproduce themselves. Luckily, the doctors were able to harvest Nicky's own stem cells back in April at the beginning of treatment so that we could use them after the chemotherapy; this is called an autologous transplant or auto transplant. It's much simpler and healthier for the patient as it lessens the chance of adverse reactions or rejection that might happen if stem cells from a donor are used. Although Dr. Rod was overseeing all of Nicky's treatments, Dr. Megan Pike was our direct point of contact throughout the stem cell transplant. She had taken time from her own IWK Halifax children's hospital to come and learn from our doctors all about stem cell transplant procedures.

When the stem cells are administered, it's extremely anticlimactic; they are injected via the IV and for some reason the room smells weird for a couple days—like onions or something. Then the cell counts begin to drop over the next few days, and the patient needs support to combat pain, nausea, and over all discomfort. Mucositis, an inflammation of the mucous membranes, can affect the throat and mouth and create hundreds of little sores all the way down the trachea. Eventually the layers of skin begin to slough off and gag the patient. It's painful and gross and there's no other way to describe it except to say it is tortuous. As this affects the throat, Nicky's voice changed, raising it a few octaves, so it sounded much higher than usual. I found it unnerving. His looks changed too, and he was unable to smile fully; it almost looked like he had had a stroke, but I knew he hadn't. The staff at BCCH were absolutely incredible trying to keep Nicky and me feeling safe and cared for throughout, but one can only do so much. He had to endure it. And we prayed it would work.

As part of the stem cell treatment, Nicky needed to have a nasogastric (NG) tube installed. This would run from his nose to his stomach and deliver nutrients directly so he could stay as strong as possible. He was not enthralled at the prospect of having this tube inserted, but a very skilled nurse who is also a friend of his, helped him to see that it would eventually make him feel better and recover faster. As we were gearing up for the procedure, I started to give him a pep talk.

"Nicky, you're back in that car. Look at the sidewalks. Who do you see? Look at how many people are chanting your name. Are you loved? Do they believe in you?"

"Yes," he nodded.

It was helping, but I could see the room to which we were bound did not feel safe to him; it was starting to spin off its axis and was filling up with heightened anticipation and worry.

"Nicky, what can you control? Your breath. You can always control your breath," I told him. He nodded and breathed in for four counts and out for four counts. With great courage, he gave the go ahead.

Our nurse was extremely capable and in less than five seconds, it was done. The feeding tube was installed. Nicky was overwhelmed by the sensation and the experience, but he held steady until the room emptied. Then all those big feelings were bestowed upon me. This was good. This trauma needed to leave his spirit. I was his safe space, and I am built to hold it all for him. An NG tube and not being able to use your day pass?! Let it out. I still wonder how it must have felt for him to constantly surrender his whole being, body and mind, in trust that we, the grownups, knew what we were doing. I am so glad the trust was there.

A while later, serendipity appeared. Nicky asked for today's package from his class. That day, the package was prepared by his bestie Ryan. He opened it with great enthusiasm and was instantly moved. He smiled with delight at his favourite comic books and a letter about strength and brotherhood.

He smiled at me. "There you are," I thought to myself.

Ultimately, Nicky pulled the NG tube out in his sleep, and we had to rely on TPN (Total Parenteral Nutrition), fed through his IV, to get him the vital nutrients. These were big bags of yellow liquid that were custom-made for each patient that needed them. Thank goodness for science.

This was one of our hardest weeks yet on the journey, but the effort of our community, both at the parade and with all the ongoing gestures of support, gave Nicky newfound strength. He truly believed that everyone was with him on that road. He saw it. He drew from it. In tough times, I could remind him of it.

Directly after the parade, my brother Ryan had to move to Halifax for a new job as a radio host with a morning show for a rock station out there. We were all excited for him to do what was best for him and his family, but it took every ounce of strength to watch him leave for the other side of the country. I promised myself I would not let my life be the reason he would need to stay. We vowed to keep tabs on each other through daily calls and texts. We would talk all the time and he would allow me to live vicariously through him during their house hunting and organizing daycare for my niece. He'd often send me clips from his radio show to entertain me and to share in his own excitement about his new job.

One day, he sent me one of these clips where he was helping to raise awareness for a fundraiser for the local children's hospital. It was organized in honour of a twelve-year-old boy named Canon who had a tumour in his abdomen.

Immediately, I responded, "Ryan, I love that you're still trying to make a difference, but honestly, just be present where you are and focus on your own local charities and needs over there."

He instantly called me back. "No! You have it wrong. There is a boy named *Canon* who is battling *cancer* right here in Halifax. His mom is named *Shelly*, and I was helping to create awareness for their fundraiser."

I was dumbfounded. Shelly and Kelly? Nicky Cannon and Canon?

Ryan and I talked for a long time about all the serendipitous moments we had experienced throughout this crazy adventure that is cancer, and he agreed that having them into the station and helping them feel like celebrities was an important part of what he could do. That fuel that we had received in the parade needed to be shared with as many kids as possible in as many ways as possible.

Since then, Shelly and I have met and become close friends and allies. Having a friend who truly understands the unique struggles that this illness creates for children is the biggest blessing. I'm so grateful for this friendship and love that we will forever have this wild story to share. And yes, our Dr. Megan Pike from Halifax worked at the same children's hospital where Canon was treated. When I shared this story with her, her jaw hit the ground and the joy of miracle moments took a deep route in our hearts to always share.

CHAPTER 18: LIVER ABLATION THERAPY

Nicky's cancer had caused several small lesions to form on his liver and while they had shrunk with chemotherapy, they could not be targeted with radiation. So, the next step in the treatment plan was liver ablation therapy—a procedure performed by an interventional radiologist who, guided by an X-ray, uses a needle-like apparatus to ablate any lesions off the liver. Dr. Steven Ho performed this procedure at VGH—Vancouver General Hospital—in November. Throughout all of Nicky's treatments, I had trained myself to only focus on what my brain could handle. We had conquered the big abdomen bump. Now we needed to take care of the cancerous lesions on his liver and hope the ones on his lungs had been eradicated by all the chemo and stem cell treatments.

Once we arrived at VGH, we had to navigate our way through the halls and try to find the correct check-in desk—it was nerve wracking. Once we had checked in, we were given scrubs and provided with a bed to wait in. Nicky looked more and more apprehensive, and I have to admit, I don't think I was my strongest self that morning. We were chatting together, aware that everyone else in the common space was significantly older, when a familiar face with a Santa hat appeared. It was Dr. Gord Finlayson who was the father of a school mate and friend of Nicky's. With an easy smile, he told us that he would be our anesthesiologist, and it brought instant relief to me and Nicky. Gord took the driver's seat and cheered us up as we pushed forward and focused on getting through this next procedure. I knew he would encourage this new and unfamiliar team at the adult hospital to stop at nothing to save my boy.

Dr. Ho came by and went through all the information and documents we would need to sign off on and made sure Nicky was comfortable and knew what to expect. As we entered the tiny room where it would all happen, a nurse a bit shorter than me looked stunned. She looked at Nicky and me and then quickly turned away, busying herself with the instruments for the procedure. As I left the room, I felt an overwhelming sense of numbness, but another friendly face soon appeared. Dr. Sarah Finlayson, Gord's wife and my friend, came and wrapped me up in a hug. It was exactly what I needed. She linked her arm in mine and led me towards the exit and across the property to her own office where I could wait until the procedure was over.

She sat me down, got me a coffee, and kept the conversation going to put me at ease. I ended up emptying my mind's thoughts onto her. I don't remember exactly what we spoke of that day; I just remember enjoying her presence and calm positivity. Her energy helped me coast through the hours while Nicky lay asleep on the table undergoing yet another procedure carried out by a skilled and talented team. And wow were they talented. Three hours later we got the call to come back as Nicky would soon wake up.

When we arrived back at the room, Dr. Ho explained that everything had gone exceptionally well. He had been able to get all the lesions, even a couple that he didn't think he'd be able to reach. I moved towards the bed where Nicky lay, and I made eye contact with the nurse. I saw that she was crying. She approached me and tearfully said, "I'm so sorry you have to go through this. He is so young. I am so so sorry." Gord explained she wasn't used to working on patients so young, and she was a new mom. I understood where she was coming from and decided to close the gap between us. She was crying openly now so I put my arm around her. I told her he was going to be just fine.

"Thank you for doing such fine work and caring so much for my sweet boy," I said. I could tell the doctors were unimpressed with her lack of professionalism, but it touched me deeply that this team cared so deeply for my child.

We moved to recovery in the ICU at VGH. A recovery at BCCH is very different from a recovery at VGH. We were shielded by curtains, but the sights and sounds outside of the realities of other people's traumas and trials in life were loud. Despite this, Nicky was treated as the most important and special patient there. Nurses continually doted on him, brushing his head, caressing his cheek, and squeezing his hand. They loved on him and enjoyed his sweet and grateful demeanor. Gord came by multiple times to make sure the medications were working the way he wanted them to for his pain. We eventually were moved back to BCCH by ambulance. Our ambulance guys were so kind and encouraging—they made him feel like a rock star.

This had been the most foreign and strange part of Nicky's treatment so far, but the staff at VGH literally held our hands and helped us find hope and grace in a scary place. I think we interacted with Dr. Ho for a total of six hours maybe—and yet those six hours literally changed our lives. His skill and talent felt like divine interactions, and we are so grateful. Sarah and Gord were also pivotal in building Nicky's courage and will be counted among his heroes forever. Their friendship was vital throughout this ordeal and an example to live up to. Selfishly, I sometimes wonder if the universe had them attend medical school and send their kids to the same school as Nicky just so they could be there for us at the exact moment and in the exact way we needed them. It's almost as if they somehow magically anticipated our need for lightning.

CHAPTER 19: RADIATION AND TATS

The next step in Nicky's treatment was a course of radiation. Early on in Nicky's chemotherapy sessions, a young lady came round and introduced herself to us to let us know she would be the doctor in charge of the upcoming radiation treatment plan. She was charming; I knew our kids had attended the same preschool and, as it turned out, her son had just applied to my youngest's school for grade 1.

When Nicky was about to start radiation, we met again, but this time, she was less personable and far more solemn. Rubbing her beautiful pregnant belly, she kept saying she would do her best, which I took to mean it might not be good enough. I knew she didn't want to make promises when she didn't know if she could keep them. No false hope. I went back to Dr. Rod and questioned if she was really the person we wanted when it seemed we didn't have the same connection that I felt with the rest of the team. He assured me that she was a genius and that she was just a "numbers person." He said that's exactly what we would want for the doctor in charge of our radiation treatment. "Okay," I thought. "I trust Rod, so I trust her."

It took some solid practice to feel safe with this portion of the treatment. I can admit that my calm was not so calm, and I finally gave in to the anxiety during the nights leading up to it. I felt the fear and dread surge over my heart and through my chest. The panic attacks began. At this point, a friend who had battled anxiety throughout their life gave me the best advice. They had struggled for years without medication and had finally decided to give it a go. They told me, begged me even, not to wait, saying that if they could have gone back in time, they would have started the medication much sooner. Lexapro had worked for them. Days later, I embarked on a relationship with Escitalopram, and it changed my life. It didn't numb me out. It allowed me to feel all the feelings, but it took the edge of panic out of it. It kept me sharp and gave my mind permission to take a step back from the panic while maintaining a laser focus. It was like I had been given my own superhero suit and a new piece of armour. I was ready for our next phase.

So, we began radiation.

When we had our first set-up meeting for radiation, I didn't know what to expect. All I had heard was that Nicky would be tattooed in three spots, and these would be used as markers; in addition, a mold would be made of his body so that he would lie down in the exact same position every time. The idea of tattoos gave me pause. I was raised to never ink my body. My parents looked down on the art form and shamed us if we even thought about it. Obviously, this was different.

As we waited in our chairs for our names to be called, I noticed another patient—an adult— who was incredibly nervous. I kept giving her smiles as I squeezed Nicky's hand in reassurance. Finally, it was our turn. We entered the small, cluttered room and were greeted by the team of technicians inside. Nicky hopped up on the table and they began the casting procedure. This was uneventful, but tedious and long as everything had to be absolutely precise. Nicky needed to lie down and grip two bars above his head. He complained his hands would go numb while maintaining the position for the team, but he obeyed and made sure to keep them where they asked.

Next came the tattoos, and the needles needed to make them. It was obvious that Nicky was nervous. They offered to do all three at once—three technicians would each work on him simultaneously. This seemed altogether worse for him, and I could see the panic developing in his eyes and body. I knew I had to do something, so I offered to show him what it would look like. They could practice on me first. He seemed to like that idea. The gal rolled up my sleeve and poked my skin with a freckle-sized dot of ink. It made me jump inside, but I'm pretty sure I looked brave in the moment. That's all that would be visible, a little, black freckle dot. Nicky agreed to do it if he could count down from ten himself and if they promised they would be fast.

And so, we left that day with a total of four tattoos between us. The rebel inside me celebrated the idea that I finally got inked! Of course, I wish we'd never had to get them in the first place, but I decided to celebrate it anyway. It was another instance of finding joy in the small victories, a diamond moment.

To this day, I love my little dot and I can't think of another design that would ever be more meaningful to me. It reminds me of where we were and that together, we made it through.

CHAPTER 20: THE FLASH

It was a weekend day in December 2021, and we were in the midst of the radiation treatments. Nicky was bored and tired of being a cancer patient. He found nothing inspiring except the comfort of watching reruns of *The Flash* and reading through his comic book collection, which had been steadily growing throughout the year thanks to his friends' care packages. I looked for anything that I could muster up that might spark his interest: board games, card tricks—and then it came to me.

"Get in the car, babe. We're going to go find The Flash."

Nicky was stunned and didn't know what I was up to. *I* didn't know what I was up to! But we got into my little Mini Cooper car anyway, and I put the top down. Nicky was wearing his favourite tie-dyed hoodie, his sky-blue cashmere beanie, and a smile from ear to ear. Off we went. I headed east, as I remembered seeing movie trucks towards that area at some point in the year. We drove along, giggling all the way. Nicky was fired up to create a miracle and some magic. We turned down the Cambie street bridge—a route I never take to get downtown. I don't know why I did that time. I took the first exit off the bridge, and on the off ramp I saw a sign attached to the lamp post and a few pieces of equipment near the curb.

"Turn left!" ordered my internal guide. So, I did. I pulled into the roundabout of a hotel and rolled the window down to speak to someone, anyone.

A gentleman approached the car, and I asked, "Are you filming *The Flash*?" He hesitated and then seeing Nicky with his sweet, thin smile and his beanie on, he confirmed that they were. We literally had driven, guided by intuition, to find the set of a hero. I explained Nicky's story briefly and politely begged if Nicky could somehow meet him or get an autograph or anything. This gentleman, Kirk, took charge and relayed the request to his producers. He returned and said nothing could happen that day, but that he would do his best and be in touch. We drove away squealing in delight and joy. Magic was in the air. Kirk had given me his business card with his contact information. *The Flash* was also emblazoned on it. We were on the right path. Lightning had struck.

Days went by and while Kirk and I played text tag, nothing concrete had been planned. Finally, I received an email from none other than Grant Gustin, The Flash himself! He and I went back and forth trying to organize a day when he and Nicky could talk. Unfortunately, at that time, Nicky was not feeling well due to the many side effects from his various treatments. In fact, though we didn't realize it yet, his liver was failing. As excited as he was, he asked if we could delay the meeting.

But then this happened: The Flash sent a video of himself on set talking directly to Nicky, cheering him on, and promising to be in touch to set up a meeting once he was feeling up to it. Nicky was in awe. Right when his body was having the hardest time recovering, this man, this character that represented bravery, sent a bolt of lightning courage directly to Nicky so that he could persevere a little more for a little longer.

Over the years, Grant has given his time and energy to Nicky and has become a friend and ally to hold onto. It's hard to describe how important and awe-inspiring this has been for Nicky. It's made a mountain of difference for his mindset. Socially, Nicky wasn't sure where he would land after all of this. But The Flash was now a real friend of his. This fact gave him a sense of calm. It gave him confidence and self-esteem. Most importantly, it gave him joy—true joy.

The team of *The Flash,* and Grant especially, changed my child's mental health and his trajectory in life because they chose to care. They didn't need to, but they did. Nicky will forever lead *The Flash* fan club, and they have an absolute ally in me. We will forever be grateful.

CHAPTER 21: CHRISTMAS

As the Christmas season approached, we all started to look forward to some traditions—some semblance of normalcy in the midst of all this medical treatment. Nicky was born on Christmas day, and throughout his childhood, the famous Elf on the Shelf has played an important role. For those who are unfamiliar, this tradition revolves around the idea that Santa sends scout elves to observe the behaviour of children and to report back on whether they have been naughty or nice. After their report, the elves return back to their house, but never to the same spot! Finding your elf in a new place every day is one of the magical joys of the Christmas season.

Once Nicky reached five years of age, our elf Jingles turned a bit mischievous. His antics played out over social media and began to attract quite a following. Jingles was always going outside the lines when he coloured our home and lives with his tricks. Now that Nicky is older, he has joined in helping Jingles surprise his younger brother, choosing to create the magic rather than be part of the audience. This tradition carried on at the hospital and throughout the COVID-19 pandemic. Nicky ensured our elves were all vaccinated and that all the hygiene protocols, including the use of sterile gloves and bandages, were followed. The impending holiday season meant it was time to find more intentional moments with our family. And Jingles, with the help of our Christmas baby Nicky, proved he was up for the challenge.

Magic has always played an important role in our family. So has the belief that the impossible is always possible. Sometimes it plays out as a funny looking elf that sits on the shelf and makes crazy punk stunts or messes in the kitchen for Mom to find. And sometimes it's because Mom is always able to spot the rainbow once the rain stops in Vancouver. However it happens, magic is real, and is even better when it's shared.

By the time Christmas 2021 arrived, we had made it through our fifteenth and final radiation session. It had been a grueling three weeks, but we got to celebrate Christmas and Nicky's thirteenth birthday at home. *We fucking made it!* As we all sat around the tree, smiling and giggling at the prospect of a new addition to our family—a golden retriever puppy who had been born that very morning— I couldn't help wondering how we got so lucky. Being here at home, all together on this day? It had seemed impossible just a few months ago, but I had held onto it as the goal. And we had triumphed. Now, we all looked forward to a whole new adventure with excitement: a new puppy to keep us busy and help us heal.

To top it all off, it was snowing that morning. It hadn't snowed on Christmas morning since Nicky had been born in 2008. To me, it seemed like the universe was giving him a second chance, a new and fresh start on life. He was being reborn. It was an opportunity to begin all over again. It's not fair that he should need to, but I thank God he has the opportunity to try. I thank God that we all do.

As the day wore on, the radiation side effects took hold and Nicky needed to sleep. His tummy was upset, so he couldn't enjoy his favourite meal of roast chicken and all the fixings. He actually got quite down emotionally as the day ended because he could not enjoy the snow—he still had the medcomp line precariously attached to his chest and it was too delicate for playing in the cold outside. Simply put, it was all a bit of a bummer for Nicky, but in my mind? Confetti! We had crossed the finish line. Onwards and upwards.

For New Year's Eve, we piled into the car and headed over to our cabin in Parksville to spend it with the cousins and grandparents on Darren's side. We were all so excited to be together that we decided to ignore the COVID-19 guidelines, which at that point advised people to keep their gatherings small and limited to their household. Everyone felt healthy and swore they had been following all the safety protocols. As we sat in the car, waiting to board the ferry, Nicky suddenly became nauseous and vomited. At the time, I didn't put it together. I thought it was car sickness. But as it turned out, Nicky had begun to experience the full force of the harsher side effects of the radiation treatments. We gave him some anti-nausea medications and tried to make the best of it.

And I'm glad we did because it was a glorious three days of our boys' laughter, endless games of Balderdash (involving totally inappropriate vocabulary), good food, music on my brand-new, white baby grand piano, and dogs everywhere causing even more laughter. Meanwhile, we continued to give Nicky medications to keep the nausea at bay. We took so many pictures of the kids all together with their grandparents. There were many jokes about who had more hair between Nicky, his dad, and his grandfather. Giggles and farts leaked constantly from the cousins' bunk room—and, of course, my husband (talk about nausea). It was a weekend to treasure. As we all packed up and headed home to the ferry, one of our relatives called and said they had started to sneeze. Hmm.

Sure enough, after we all arrived home, one by one we all tested positive for COVID. Fuck! Luckily, we were all asymptomatic. But, as the week progressed, Nicky began to sleep more and more. We monitored him from home but checked in with his doctors constantly. And then, the knowing—*that superior knowing*. I saw it. He returned from the bathroom shirtless, and as he got back into bed, there it was. His belly button appeared to be swollen shut. Nothing else looked odd. Both Darren and Nicky said they thought it looked fine, but my gut was screaming, "Pay attention!"

So, I packed our familiar bag and got Nicky into the car as my thumbs moved across my phone to email our team at the hospital. They were ready for us when we arrived. We were admitted and, as we had each tested positive for COVID with an antigen test, they confirmed our infections with PCR tests, and then immediately put both of us into isolation. Neither of us could leave now. At least during the stem cell transplant, I could come and go occasionally and grab a coffee from the coffee maker on the ward. Now, we were completely dependent on the good will of nurses and friends to get us anything from the outside.

Nicky underwent a series of tests, and the team finally concluded that this had nothing to do with COVID. After thirteen chemotherapy treatments, a stem cell transplant, thirteen surgeries, liver ablation therapy, and radiation, his liver was not doing well. It had gone into failure and needed its own treatment to rebuild and restore itself. The team explained that his liver had become sponge-like and wasn't functioning the way it should, which is why his abdomen was so swollen. We were advised to limit the amount of liquid he consumed, measuring down to the drop, and in yet another procedure, they drained the fluid that had collected in his body. I wondered when Nicky's liver would recover, but the doctors said, "It just takes time."

We were on such a short leash with drinks that even the ice we gave him counted. I got crafty. I figured if we could only have one drink, we might as well make it a good one! I asked Darren to bring me bartending tools and we made Shirley Temples with little umbrellas and maraschino cherries on plastic swords. We would toast to each other and use a flashlight in the window to signal over to VGH where Nicky's grandfather had been admitted with COVID. We figured we could communicate via morse code with him. He was on the geriatric ward, and we would Facetime with him as well and chat about our days. He was improving and it lifted our spirits to see him get better. In our corner suite, T8-109, we played UNO and watched *Superstore*, a fabulous TV show that made everyone laugh.

As isolation dragged on, we engaged with Nicky's tutor team for school and began to get back to some light schoolwork. At night, when he would go to sleep, I would stare out of our corner window and enjoy the view of the city lights. Christmas, when I had felt so victorious, seemed like months ago—not days. I remembered feeling that we had won, and it was over. And yet here we were again. It was hard not to feel disheartened, but I tried to stay focused. "This is just a curveball," I told myself.

Finally, after we had been in isolation in the hospital almost a month, Nicky's tests started to show some improvement. At last, he could enjoy a full glass of water! Eventually, and uneventfully, we were discharged and returned home. It was, in fact, just another curveball that the universe pitched us. Maybe it thought we weren't ready to bunt back. But we did. We had gotten really smooth in handling those curve balls. If it were up to me, I think I could actually pitch a few myself.

Now the real healing began. Nicky met with his tutors every day for an hour or so. They started with lessons from a couple of grade levels below where he actually had left off to rebuild his confidence and not overwhelm him. It was going to take some getting used to. For the entire time that Nicky was undergoing treatment, we did not study once. We had forfeited academics for survival. So now, as Nicky began to transition back into a more normal life, we took baby steps, allowing him some space to get used to it all again. Fortunately, he always had a mathematical brain, and he loved being at the head of the class and leading the group towards the next lesson. He wanted to get back to that place.

There was much sleep needed, for both of us. Rest helps a person heal physically, but also mentally. We were drained in every way, and especially felt a deficit in terms of emotional energy. We both needed to just zone out sometimes. As weird as it seemed, it was necessary to simply do nothing and just relax. I did this by watching TV and movies, practicing meditation and Reiki, playing piano, listening to music, and writing. Nicky found gaming helpful throughout the experience in the hospital, and he continued to turn to it after we went home. It allowed him to be social with friends without having to physically be with them, something he couldn't do when he was in the hospital, and something he sometimes found he didn't have enough energy for after he was home.

Physiotherapy helped Nicky to gradually ease into regular social interactions. Eventually, he worked up to attending school events, where he remembered that being social was fun! It was exciting to watch all his friendships rekindle organically. He and Clive also had to get reacquainted. They had been separated for a long time, but they had always shared a room, and that wasn't going to change. Now they were back together again, they needed to set new boundaries with each other and figure out how to connect with respect on a daily basis. I don't want to pretend that this was a seamless process, or that somehow, we have figured out how to get kids to always like each other. If we had, that would be the subject of my next book! We were all a bit sensitive to the light, so to speak, after being in the dark for so long. But we were also now all experts in patience and being uncomfortable, so thankfully, we gradually acclimatized.

CHAPTER 22: SCANXIETY

It was February 22, 2022. 2-22-22: "Twosday"—scan day. People had told me about "scanxiety," and I had upped my anti-anxiety medication in anticipation. However, in the lead up, I hadn't been feeling the discomfort of not knowing. On the contrary, I'd been calm, steady, and joyful. The week before Nicky's appointment for his scan, where we would find out if he really was in the clear, we were in Parksville. There, I had delighted in the beautiful way the light weaved through the trees. I could see the enthusiastic energy from the sea lions surfing in the sea foam as the white caps toppled onto the shore of Rathtrevor beach. I saw how Nicky's freckles on his forehead formed a constellation like Cassiopeia. I held my sweet child in my arms as his moods continued to swing from delight to frustration. "Yes, I can!" to "*Why* is this still so hard?" I saw his spirit fall when math seemed complicated, and he lost his confidence in an instant. I saw it come back when he found another way to be passionate, creative, and confident through cooking. I saw it all.

I kept my eyes on his on this day, but as they wheeled Nicky into the MRI, we briefly lost contact. As the MRI machine beeped and buzzed, he tuned out to a movie, *Captain Marvel*, and I closed my eyes to feel my thoughts, the energy of my gaze running through my closed lids. One word: *clear*. I don't think I have ever been so calm and so singular in my thoughts, but I guess I'd say it wasn't even my thoughts. It was the knowing. It was the strongest meditation I have ever been able to hold—and the longest for sure. I felt our guides and angels all around us, assuring us that everything will be clear, that we would be safe.

And they *were* clear! Clear scans rewarded our steady belief in magic. We had finally crossed the finish line of this marathon of suffering and worry, and we had *won!* We had beaten cancer and left it in the dust. The sense of relief was so profound, I find it difficult to put it into words.

Later that week, we arrived at the clinic with Clive in tow to finally get Nicky's medcomp line removed. Here we stood, together as a unit. Nicky was excited to finally see the oncology procedure room that I had bragged about during my volunteer years. It was created with help from the Vancouver Planetarium and was meant to be a place where kids could lose themselves in the stars. At the entry, there is a "get ready and suit up" theme to the wall decoration. Space suits and badges of honour are depicted to inspire the courage that will be required for the expedition. When you enter the procedure room, you realize that the lighting isn't like the other operating rooms. It's dimly lit to help create a sense of calm. As the patient lies down and peers upwards, they see that the ceiling is painted a dark navy blue and within it are lights that, when activated, reveal the constellations visible in Vancouver's sky. When the procedure is complete, the patient is moved into recovery next door, which is again lit with special lights to emulate the aurora borealis. The patient is given a remote to dim or raise the light levels to signal to the nurses whether they are waking up or still need more rest.

Nicky sat down and began to suit up like a spaceman, but with a hospital gown instead. Once he had changed, in walked our general surgeon, Dr. Webber. Throughout this whole expedition, from the initial biopsy to the removal of the tumour, he had taken a special interest in Nicky. He had always stopped in to cheerfully say hello, genuinely checking in to make sure Nicky stayed steadily on the road to recovery. He was going to be the one to make sure the line came out safely. I took some photos of Nicky and him together while Clive toured the area with the nurse—he was fascinated by the whole thing. When Nicky eventually got on the table and started to go to sleep, Clive finally got to be the one by his side, telling him he loved him and holding his hand. Nicky tried all his tricks to stay awake and impress his younger brother, but to their delight, he didn't make it very long.

When Nicky awoke, we all felt the freedom of finally being released from that tethering line. No longer would he need to be hooked up to medicines. A tiny bandage was the only evidence that there had been anything there at all.

I am so grateful to Dr. Webber and his devotion to his work with children. I am inspired by him and indebted to him for being so diligent and encouraging in caring for my child and family. We truly feel a deeply rooted connection and everlasting friendship with him and thank him from the bottom of our hearts.

CHAPTER 23: LEAD WITH LOVE

In April 2023, Clive received an award from his hockey league—by reputation, the most prestigious award they give out. A player has to be nominated by the coaches for it. It is called the Mitchell Ho Memorial Award. It is in honour and memory of the Ho family's son who loved hockey and was always a bright spot on the team, a kid you were happy to see and share a pass or laugh with. He passed away as a result of a heart problem at eleven years old in 1997. His family created the award as a legacy and a way to keep his memory alive.

Nicky and I were there for the ceremony, and we cheered excitedly as Clive—bashful yet proud—went up to accept the giant trophy. After, he walked over to meet Mitchell's dad. They shook hands, and Clive thanked him. The man looked down at Clive and politely said, "Congratulations, Clive. It's nice to meet you." Clive was beaming and the moment looked equally important to this father. He then turned to Nicky and said, "Nicky, it's nice to see you out of a stretcher." I initially smiled in response, and then froze, stunned by what he had said.

"I'm sorry? I asked puzzled. This gentleman looked at me and extended his hand. It wrapped warmly around my own nervous hand as I put the pieces together and began to finally recognize our doctor without his COVID face mask on.

He turned to Nicky who was looking equally as puzzled, and said, "Nicky, I am your doctor. I'm the one who worked on your liver. I didn't know Clive was your brother!"

Tearfully, we giggled and laughed and chatted. It turned out that he now worked two days a week at the children's hospital. This was partly due to Dr. Heron's influence, but rumor has it, it was also because of the experience of having Nicky as a patient. Again, the serendipity, the lightning, struck.

We think we are in control of our lives. The biggest lesson I have learned through this crazy time is that we are in control of nothing. That can seem overwhelming and scary, but if you surrender to it, you will find that wherever you are, if you stay in the moment and focus on what you can control, you can get through anything. If lightning strikes, you can survive. The one thing you can always rely on is your breath. Focus on the next breath and you have made it to the next moment. Life gets shrunk into these fragments when illness strikes you and your family. You can find strength in those moments by realizing you have already survived all of your worst days to date and that you have a community behind and beside you ready to help. It may be the community you live in, it may be the community of people you meet in the hospital or health centres, or it may be people you've never even met but suddenly appear to help. These people will make themselves known. Notice them when they come along. Serendipitous things happen, and they can help you if you pay attention to the lightning.

The truth is that one day, everyone will have a story that brings them to their knees. Maybe it's when you lose a parent. Maybe a marriage or relationship ends, or a career fails, or financially you get taken down. Maybe your own health fails, or your child is hit with an illness that knocks you off your feet. Nobody gets out of this without an injury of some sort to their spirit. But I've learned that scars tell stories; they are life's very own badass tattoos. The more you have, the more stories you can share and the more proof of life you have. I don't want to die without scars. I say, let them add up all over my spirit and body. They are evidence of healing, resilience, and growth.

I could give you all the scary statistics about how many marriages survive this kind of situation (it's a very low number), what the financial implications can be, how many friendships are lost, and how many are gained. I could provide the percentages on how many children respond to the treatments.

Here's what I need to say to all of that: You are not a statistic. You are you, special and unique. Although statistics can guide the experts in the medical field as to how to treat the science behind your illness, they do not dictate how your own mind will handle it, or how you will experience it, or how you will respond to it. That's all up to you. And there is no failure in this. No one fails at cancer. The only failure is not to try. The only failure is not to see the gifts it can bring to your life. It gives you the moments. It gives you the ability to wake up and pay attention to the spinning world around you, to find your footing, and to focus your lens on what is truly important. It allows you the excuse, if you need one, to slow down and perhaps rediscover what you may have lost sight of: love, connections, relationships, trust, and loyalty. It allows you to be true to your authentic self, and to validate that authentic self. And ultimately, it allows you to serve the ones who need it the most.

When he was diagnosed, Nicky was on the cusp of becoming an eye-rolling teenager who was too cool for his parents. Because of this illness, he and I now have an unshakeable bond and he knows that I will always provide a safe space for him. For that, I am grateful. I have watched in absolute awe of our "Uncle Rod" through this grueling process as he cared for all of us, and for so many other families at the same time. I have met no better human than Dr. Rod Rassekh. My greatest lessons in life have been learned as a result of his care. For that, I am also grateful.

I can even find gratitude in what this experience did for my marriage. This illness pushed Darren and me to the absolute edge, to our breaking point, but somehow, we got through it together. And while things might not be perfect, the survival of our relationship through this ordeal is still something important that I hang onto. After enduring a pandemic and a cancer diagnosis, our marriage came out limping at best. It has taken time for us to align again. It is still, and will always be, a work in progress. We resumed our marriage counselling, and I am so grateful to say we are both committed to the best outcome for both of us. For now, we continue to work on things together in couples counselling and individually with our own therapists. Finally, after having space to grieve and to celebrate, finding time to prioritize our relationship is, in itself, a victory. I am so grateful to our friends and families who have supported us and helped keep us on track throughout this.

For Darren and me, navigating the complexities of childhood cancer has been an immense challenge. Yet, the decision to actively work on our marriage is deeply significant. It serves as a crucial source of emotional support during the most trying moments, reinforcing our resilience as a family. That commitment not only plays a pivotal role in Nicky and Clive's ongoing recovery, but also nurtures a stronger bond between us, creating a sense of unity that positively impacts our individual well-being amid life's greatest adversities. Again, the only failure is not to try. We went through hell together, but we did not give up. We survived, and that fact has only made us stronger.

You need not fear death. Spoiler alert: it ends the same for everyone at some point. What matters is what you do in the middle. I'm sure we've all heard that it's the dash between your birthday and your last day that is what matters, no matter how big or how small it ends up being. This was my story—the one that brought me to my knees. This is what I learned:

- ✦ Don't lead with fear, lead with love. Fear is the opposite of love, so set your focus correctly. It will set the tone for your journey.
- ✦ Find your breath in the hardest times. Breathe one breath at a time; it's the one thing we can truly control. With every breath is a small victory of yet one more moment.
- ✦ Listen to your intuition, your gut. You know your kid best, and the team will tell you the same.
- ✦ Look for the signs. Lightning and hummingbirds, finding white feathers and seeing 11:11 flash on your clock—whatever signs you see that are magical to you, treat them as evidence that you are not alone on this journey, and that your guides are there to protect you.
- ✦ Appreciate the hurt felt by all involved, especially your partner.
- ✦ If you don't know how to respond, go with kindness.
- ✦ *Lean in*. Lean into the hurt. Let it pass through you instead of letting it happen to you. You can hold more than you think but you don't need too. Simply acknowledge the hurt and feel it move through your own energy, and then replace it with love.
- ✦ Get a really good catcher's mitt for those curve balls and be ready for some overtime.
- ✦ And finally, when you are in your darkest hours and can't see the light, please realize that the light is you. You are the brightness in

the dark. If you can't sense this, then find a way to serve. By taking your eyes off yourself and putting them on someone else, it is my opinion and experience that you will find all you need by helping someone else to survive. By serving you create magic. You will see your own light like lightning. It will appear like a powerful, room-filling glow that can change a moment with a sudden strike and unleash a captivating force that can instantaneously illuminate the darkest corners of life with an unimaginable magic and above all, the steadiness that is love.

Today, as I finish writing this, Nicky has been cancer free for nearly two years, and I celebrate every day. He started a new school and has enjoyed getting back to discovering who he is and who he wants to become. Yes, there have been consequences from the treatments, mentally and physically, but those details are his to share, not mine. Clive is still my Hammy and enjoys bossing his mama around the hockey rink. I love that I have these moments with both of them and that for a pocket of time, the water has been calm and the skies clear. I understand that one day, something else will come at us, but these moments we have shared as a family, as friends, and as a community have given us the strength, the tools, and the wisdom to be able to face anything.

I hope this book illuminates the intricate tapestry of life and how its events can unfold with the unpredictable force of a lightning strike. With each chapter, I've tried to reveal the profound impact of choices and underline that the consequences of those choices shape our destinies in unexpected and sometimes electrifying ways. It was through my experience with pediatric cancer that I gained a deeper understanding of the interconnectedness and resonating effects that, like lightning, have left an indelible mark on my own existence. I am so grateful for all of it.

I'll finish with the words that I used to meditate on when I felt I could not go on:

> *The wind whispered in her ear, "You'll never survive the storm." She whispered back, "I am the storm."*

Be the storm and let the lightning strike. You've got this.

EPILOGUE

As I proudly put the finishing touches on this book, the BCCH Foundation approached my family with a request that exemplifies the idiosyncratic, magical serendipity of my entire experience with the pediatric oncology floor. They asked us to help establish an endowed hospital chair in support of the clinical side of the oncology ward. Endowed chairs, like the Team Nicky Hospital Chair in Hematology, Oncology and Blood & Marrow Transplant, are among the most prestigious academic and clinical appointments in Canada, reserved for internationally recognized researchers, teachers, and clinicians. Usually, this honour is reserved for a family that can give a substantial donation, but the uniqueness of Nicky's story and the community that rallied around him gave them an idea. They wanted to have our family, Team Nicky, lead the effort to raise four million dollars that the BCCH Foundation will match with one million dollars. This fund will forever be banked and untouched. The interest made will be used, at the discretion of the Chair, to allow for the development of proactive, preventive, and cutting-edge treatments with an emphasis on compassion. The Team Nicky Chair is to be the voice for the patients in the oncology ward, those undergoing the clinical and bedside treatments, to ensure we are one step ahead of whatever is needed by whoever walks through the doors.

As I write this, the BCCH oncology ward is reeling from a series of devastating losses. These weren't just statistics, they were families we travelled down this road together with, people who became our friends, children we knew and loved. These losses highlight a stark reality: childhood cancer is not a distant, future problem; it's a pressing, urgent matter that demands our immediate attention. The pain is raw and the need for action is critical. As we share the burden of grief with these families, we feel an undeniable call to action. Team Nicky will forever be committed to making a difference in the lives of those who are currently battling cancer and those who one day will.

It is no coincidence that I have been witnessing the magic and fight of the children on this ward since I was an adolescent. It was no coincidence that Nicky made it out of that ward as famously as he did. It would never be my wish for Nicky or our family to endure what we have, but we did, and now we have the privilege and obligation to ensure that no one is left behind. So, we accepted the honour and have committed to raising the funds. We want these resilient young warriors to have every tool possible at their disposal so they can fight their fight successfully and know they are not in this alone. They have the entire community of Team Nicky standing beside them, ensuring they have what it takes to win, both inside themselves and within the walls of our hospital. And they have us to lean on. We'll help them catch every curveball coming their way and realize they are on the winning team—Team Nicky.

ACKNOWLEDGEMENTS

I'd like to thank some of the people involved in bringing this book to life. I'll begin with the team at BC Children's Hospital. I am deeply grateful to the entire oncology department as well as the many teams of specialists we needed along the way there and at Vancouver General Hospital, from general surgery to anesthesia and pain management, nephrology, hepatology, diagnostic and interventional radiology, and all of the dedicated professionals from the floors 3, 4, 6, and 8 at BCCH and the ERs, ICUs, and ambulance services at both hospitals. The care, kindness, and unending support we were shown from all of the staff at these hospitals allowed for our world to continue. I am also grateful to the BC Cancer radiation team.

To our schools, their faculty, student bodies, and parent communities: you carried us through moments I didn't want to experience. You came along with us and made sure we knew we weren't alone.

To my sisters by blood, law, energy, and choice: I love you forever.

To our families, our parents, siblings, in-laws, nieces, and nephews: we would not be who we are today without you.

To Jing Credo, our incredible babysitter turned nanny in the hardest of times: you held our family together with your love and prayers, and I'm so grateful. You are forever an honorary Cannon.

To my editor, Alison: thank you for coming along on this ride and ensuring my words match my thoughts and intentions. You have been so incredibly patient with me—a true guide enabling me to present this experience for others to witness.

To my designer, Angela: I love that you understood visually how I hoped this would appear.

To my PR and communications leader and now dear friend, Anna: I'm so grateful for your truth, your heart, and friendship. Your ability and talent to help me navigate this journey will forever be how I wish to help others in life. You are a serendipitous life treasure.

To Megan and Ira: your experience in this industry is second to none. I'm so grateful our paths crossed and we formed this partnership. It's been an experience I'll never forget, and I look forward to doing more in the future with you.

Lastly, to the mothers, fathers, and caregivers who allowed me to come along for their own pediatric cancer journeys when I was a volunteer: the wisdom and light you brought to the hallways and rooms of the original 2B and 3B and then to our new building on the 8th floor at BCCH enabled me to carry my son through the trenches. From the bottom of my heart, thank you.

Family Portrait Photography | Kathryn PBK

ABOUT THE AUTHOR

Writer, speaker, and philanthropist Kelly Cannon has made giving back a defining principle of her life. Her advocacy journey began in her teenage years as she volunteered in the oncology ward after witnessing the profound toll childhood cancer took on the family of a dear friend. However, it was her own son, Nicky, who faced a rare pediatric cancer diagnosis in March 2021, who ignited her unwavering commitment to the cause.

Empowered by the support of her community and inspired by Nicky's bravery during his treatments, Kelly emerged as a guiding light for families grappling with childhood illness. She took to social media to share her insights on courage, gratitude, and hope using her signature brand of compassion and optimism. With giving back at the forefront of her heart, Kelly later embarked on a mission to create a community-driven chair for BC Children's Hospital's oncology and hematology clinical department, known as Team Nicky.

Symbolized by the iconic reverse lightning bolt, the Team Nicky chair and fundraising arm will bring innovative research initiatives from around the globe and access to immediate funding capabilities for cutting-edge treatments. More than that, for patients of BC Children's Hospital, it will serve as a symbol of Kelly's belief that courage is not something we wear as a mask, hiding our true feelings and challenges behind forced positivity and fake smiles; rather, courage is the strength we build in ourselves when we feel held by others. It is a product of our community—planted, grown, and nurtured by the actions of our supporters.

Kelly's debut book and ongoing philanthropy form that very support system, offering immediate strength and inspiration to the extraordinary children and families who, every day, transform their fear into love as they confront the seemingly insurmountable.